Printed in China

CCTV

快乐中国——学汉语
Happy China-Learning Chinese

《快乐中国——学汉语》节目组 编

四川篇

北京语言大学出版社

前　言

中国的发展令世人瞩目。随之而来的外国人学汉语热潮也在全球范围内兴起。

中国中央电视台国际频道(CCTV-4)的《快乐中国—— 学汉语》栏目，通过与中国各地城市以及风景名胜点的合作，把饱览名山大川、感受中华民族历史文化与学习汉语结合起来，把掌握语言技能与知识性、趣味性和欣赏性融为一体，办成了独特的寓教于乐的电视教学节目。

在中央电视台覆盖全球98%的强势传媒下，《快乐中国—— 学汉语》自2004年6月播出以来，引起了海内外观众的热烈反响。其中，不少观众来信来电，希望能得到《快乐中国—— 学汉语》播出节目的文字和音像材料，作为学习汉语的辅助教材。为了满足广大观众的需要，北京语言大学出版社承担了这套文字、声像教材的出版编辑任务。在此，我们深表感谢！

语言是桥梁；电视是桥梁；《快乐中国—— 学汉语》同样是桥梁。它把汉语教学搬进大自然的课堂之中，"快乐学汉语，轻松又好记"。此外，我们采用高清晰电视技术和立体声制作的表现手段，充分展示汉语言中特有的内在魅力。

为了使节目主持人对话能更好地帮助您学说中国话，我们聘请了北京语言大学几位长期从事对外汉语教学和英语教学的教授，对每一集对话进行加工，增添了生词、注释、替换练习和会话等部分，并负责生词和注释部分的英文翻译。每一集生词8~10个，帮助学习者更好地理解对话内容，掌握重点句；既有模仿练习也有交际性的活用练习。在书的后部还附有全部的重点句。

为了适应读者需要，我们每册收入15集节目，并配有各个拍摄点的简介和图片。由于我们节目制作还在进行之中，今后还将陆续出版。因观众学习要求不尽相同，书中不足之处在所难免，希望得到您的指正和建议，以便今后做得更好。

《快乐中国——学汉语》栏目组

2005 年 5 月

PREFACE

The development of China has attracted the world's attention, as a result of which a great upsurge for learning Chinese has been going strong throughout the world.

Happy and Joyful China–Learning Chinese by CCTV offers learners an opportunity to learn Chinese language and culture while enjoying the beautiful scenic spots in China. Co-operating with local TV stations and the administrative section of well-known scenic spots, this program well combines language skills with the learning of Chinese culture and history in an interesting, informative and enjoyable way.

With a TV coverage of 98% of the area in the world, this program has received warm applauses from viewers home and abroad since the program was broadcast in June, 2005. Quite a few of the viewers hope that we could provide language materials as a learning aid. As a consideration of such, we have invited Beijing Language and Culture University Press, a leading press in publications on teaching foreigners Chinese, to publish these language materials for our viewers.

Apart from the language materials that appear in the program, we have included a Vocabulary List, Notes, Substitution Exercise and Conversation in each book, all of which are accompanied with brief English translations or explanations. Key sentences are presented as well. Each book is composed of 15 episodes of the TV program with brief introductions and photos of the corresponding scenic spots. As more episodes of *Happy and Joyful China–Learning Chinese* are coming up, accordingly more books will be published in this series.

Happy and Joyful China–Learning Chinese Group

九寨沟风景名胜区

被誉为"童话世界"的九寨沟位于中国四川省阿坝藏族羌族自治州境内的九寨沟县中南部，是长江水系嘉陵江白水河的一条支沟，因景区内有荷叶、树正、则渣洼等九个藏族村寨而得名。游览区海拔2000米至3100米，气候宜人，冬无寒风，夏季凉爽，四季美丽，是世界上旅游环境最佳的景区之一。九寨沟风景区于1992年被列入《世界自然遗产名录》；1997年被纳入世界人与生物圈保护区。

九寨沟，这方充满梦幻与诗意的童话世界，是自然造化赐予人类最美丽的乐土，是我们回归自然的精神家园。

Jiuzhaigou Scenic Area

Reputed as the "wonderland of fairy tales", Jiuzhaigou is located in Jiuzhaigou County, central south of Aba Autonomous Prefecture of Tibetan and Qiang Nationalities, Sichuan Province, China. It is a branch gully from the Jialing River, a ramification of the Yangtze River. It is so named because there are nine Tibetan villages such as Heye, Shushing and Peshawar, etc. The scenic area has an elevation from 2,000 to 3,100 meters. The climate is pleasant whole year round, thus it is one of the world's best tourist scenic spots. In 1992, Jiuzhaigou Scenic Area was included into the Directory of World Cultural Heritages. In 1977, it was approved as a world nature reserve.

Jiuzhaigou, a wonderland full of dreams and fairy tales, is the land gifted by nature and the spiritual home for mankind.

黄龙风景名胜区

　　黄龙地处东经102°38'－104°15'、北纬32°05'－33°09'之间，主要由黄龙主景区和丹云峡、红星岩、雪宝鼎、牟尼沟等外围景区（点）以及松潘古城组成，总面积达1340平方公里，以彩池、滩流、雪山、峡谷、森林五绝著称于世。三千多个大小不等的串珠状彩池，呈梯田状层层叠叠逶迤而下，莹红漾绿，泻翠流金。形成八个彩池群落，婉若金色巨龙身上的鳞片，闪烁出各种奇幻的色彩，艳丽诡谲，被誉为"圣地仙境、人间瑶池"。

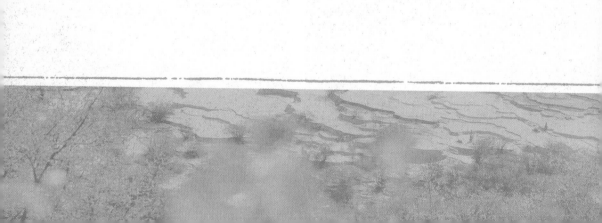

Huanglong Scenic Area

Huanglong Scenic Area, with the coordinates of 102°38' to 104°15' E and 32°05' to 30°09' N, is about 300 kilometers from Chengdu. It comprises the main scenic area and other tourist spots like Danyunxia, hongxingyan, Xuebaoding, Mounigou and ancient town of Songpan. Covering a total area of 1,340 square kilometers, Huanglong Scenic Area is best known for its "Five Wonders", namely: colored ponds, river beaches, snow mountains, and canyons and forests. More than 3,000 pearl-like colorful ponds in eight groups at different levels resemble the scales of a giant golden dragon, glittering with fantastic lights. Hence Huanglong scenic area is affectionately called the "holy wonderland and Heavenly Palace on earth".

峨眉山景区

　　峨眉山位于中国四川西南部，最高峰万佛顶海拔 3099 米。峨眉山经过了八亿年的孕育，七千万年的成长，二百万年的春风时雨，潜移默化，巍然屹立在辽阔的中国大地上。它以自然风光优美、植物种类繁多，佛教文化浓郁而驰名中外。以其"雄、秀、神、奇"的特色，1996 年 12 月被联合国教科文组织列入《世界文化与自然遗产名录》。

　　峨眉山有"高凌五岳"之称。云海、日出、佛光、圣灯是金顶四大奇观。峨眉山"一山有四季，十里不同天"。瞬息万变的形态美，神奇的动态美，绚丽的色彩美和优雅的听觉美，交织在一起，形成超凡脱俗的意境美。

Mt. Emei Scenic Area

Mt. Emei is located in the southwest of Sichuan Province, China. The highest peak Wanfoding is 3,099 meters above sea level. Having gone through 872 million years of evolving process, Mt. Emei erects straight on the land of China. It is best known at home and abroad for its beautiful natural landscape, various species of plants, and long-standing Buddhist culture. Characterized by its grandeur, elegance, mysteries and uniqueness, Mt. Emei earned its place in the Directory of World Cultural and Natural Heritages in December of 1996.

Mt. Emei is regarded as the highest of the Five Holy Mountains. The four wonders-the sea of clouds, sight of sunrise, Buddhist Halo and Holy lights can be seen atop the Golden Summit. Mt. Emei has four seasons in a day and different weathers within ten li. One can feel the sense of beauty of Mt. Emei by enjoying the ever-changing sceneries, the colorful shades and beautiful sounds of nature.

乐山大佛景区

　　乐山大佛景区位于岷江、青衣江、大渡河三江汇流处，是世界文化与自然遗产。景区面积17.88平方公里，人文景观和自然景观独具特色。这里有世界最大摩崖石刻弥勒坐像——乐山大佛、自然和人文奇观——"巨型睡佛"、青衣别岛——乌尤寺、东汉麻浩崖墓、佛教艺术荟萃——东方佛都、宋元古战场遗址——三龟九顶城。

　　景区依山傍水，风光旖旎，名胜古迹星罗棋布，恰似天然画卷，美不胜收。或拾阶登临，或游江观瞻，荡漾于青山绿水间、浸润于诗情画意中，令人心旷神怡，流连忘返。

Leshan Giant Buddha Scenic Area

Located at the junction of the Min River, Qingyi River and Dadu River, Leshan Giant Buddha Scenic Area is a world cultural and natural heritage. The scenic area covers 17.88 square kilometers and has many attractions such as the Giant Buddha of Leshan-the world's biggest stone sitting Buddha statue, the Giant Sleeping Buddha which is a miraculous work by nature and man, the Wuyou Temple on the Isolated Hill, the Mahao Cliff niches dated back to the Eastern Han dynasty, the Oriental Capital of Buddhism with a collection of Buddhist arts and the ruins of ancient battlefield in Yuan and Song Dynasties.

Surrounded by hills and rivers, dotted with historical and cultural relics, this area resembles a natural scroll of landscape paintings. Drifting on the river or climbing up the mountain steps will surely make you feel extremely relaxed and happy.

目录

CONTENTS

九寨沟

【第一集】

九寨沟沟口

韩　佳：今天，我们来到了四川的九寨沟。这里有九个藏族的村寨，"九寨沟"因此而得名。

大　牛："九"就是 *nine*，"村寨"就是 *village*，"山沟"就是 *mountain valley*，所以九寨沟就是有九座村寨的山沟。

Han Jia: Today we arrived at Jiuzhaigou of Sichuan Province. There are nine Tibetan villages here. That's how Jiuzhaigou got its name.

Daniel: "Jiu" means nine, "cunzhai" meams village, and "shangou" means mountain valley. So Jiuzhaigou is a mountain valley with nine villages.

韩 佳：哎，大牛，你看这标志，这弯的代表是山，这底下这个卷的代表是水。

大 牛：我看它倒像一只眼睛。

韩 佳：你想像力很丰富嘛。这就是说，要把天下的美景尽收眼底，而且提醒我们，要像保护眼睛一样保护环境。①

Wǒmen yào xiàng bǎohù yǎnjing yī yàng bǎohù huánjìng.

我们 要 像 保护 眼睛 一样 保护 环境。

We should protect the environment with the same care as we protect our eyes.

韩 佳：要像保护眼睛一样保护环境。

大 牛：说得好，不过你看，那么多车进进出出的，它们一定制造了不少空气污染。

韩 佳：这是绿色环保观光车。

大 牛：环保观光车？什么叫"环保"？

韩 佳："环保"就是环境保护的简称。我们生活中也经常用简称啊，你看，比如我们平时把地下铁路叫做"地铁"，把城市管理叫做"城管"。

大 牛：哦，我明白了。"环境"就是 environment，"保护"就是 to protect，那么"环保"就是 environmental protection。

韩 佳：没错。

大 牛：走吧。

Han Jia: Hey, Daniel, look at this sign. The curve represents a mountain and the roll below represents water.

Daniel: I think it's more like an eye.

Han Jia: You have rich imagination. That means it will cover all the beautiful sceneries in the world. Besides, it also reminds us to protect the environment just as we protect our eyes.

Han Jia: We should protect the environment just like protecting our eyes.

Daniel: Right. But look, there are so many vehicles coming and going. They must have caused a lot of air pollution.

Han Jia: These are green environment-friendly tour wagons.

Daniel: Environment-friendly tour wagons? What is "huanbao"?

Han Jia: "Huanbao" is short for "huanjing baohu" (environmental protection). We often use abbreviation in daily conversations. For example, we abbreviate "dixia tielu" to "ditie" (underground railway)and "chengshi guanli" to "chengguan" (municipal administration).

Daniel: Oh, I see. "Huanjing" means environment, "baohu" means to protect. So "huanbao" means environmental protection.

Han Jia: Right.

Daniel: Let's go.

环保观光车上

大　牛：看看这些山，这些湖，还没看清楚，车就开过去了。
韩　佳：大牛，你想不想和九寨美景来一次亲密接触啊？
大　牛：谁不想啊？②
韩　佳：那一会儿你有的是机会了。③

栈　道

大　牛：走在这个木板搭起的小路上挺舒服啊。
韩　佳：哦，这个叫栈道。
大　牛：栈道。A wooden walkway。你看，它还是悬空的呢。
韩　佳：这样，就不会破坏地上的植物了，可以让它们自由地生长。④
大　牛：看来，这里还真是处处体现环保精神。

Zhè li　chùchù　tǐ xiàn　huánbǎo　jīngshén.
这里　处处　体现　环保　精神。
The environmental awareness is evident in all of our surroundings.

大　牛：你听，你听，哗哗地，这么大的流水声。
韩　佳：哦，一定是到了珍珠滩了。
大　牛：啊，珍珠？这里还有珍珠？
韩　佳：有啊，而且有成千成万颗呢。
大　牛：啊，赶快去捡吧。

Daniel: Look at these mountains and these lakes. I could hardly see the scenery clearly because the vehicle runs too fast.

Han Jia: Daniel, do you want to take a closer look at the beautiful Jiuzhaigou?

Daniel: Of course, we all want.

Han Jia: Then, you will have ample opportunities later.

Daniel: It is very comfortable to walk on the path paved with wooden planks.

Han Jia: Oh, this is called "zhandao".

Daniel: A wooden walkway. You see, it's suspended in the air.

Han Jia: This way, it won't damage the plants on the ground, allowing them to grow freely.

Daniel: It seems the environmental awareness is evident everywhere here.

Daniel: Listen, what a big gurgling sound of flowing water.

Han Jia: Oh, we must have arrived at Pearl Beach.

Daniel: What, pearls? There are even pearls here?

Han Jia: Yes. And there are even tens of hundreds of them.

Daniel: Wow, let's go to pick them.

场景 珍珠滩瀑布

韩 佳：大牛，你看这个溅起来的水珠像不像一粒粒的珍珠？

大 牛：在阳光下真像是珍珠在跳跃。哎，韩佳，我想起来了我学过的一句诗，"大珠小珠落玉盘"，形容这里的景色再合适不过。⑤

韩 佳：九寨沟里面的美景还多着呢，⑥来这一趟你回去岂不成诗人了？⑦

Jiǔ zhàigōu lǐ miàn de měijǐng hái duō zhe ne.
九寨沟 里面 的 美景 还 多 着 呢。

There are still many more scenic spots to be seen in Jiuzhaigou.

韩 佳：九寨沟里面的美景还多着呢，来这一趟你回去岂不成诗人了？

大 牛：啊，那还不赶快去嘛。

韩 佳：别急嘛，汉语要一点一点地学，美景要慢慢地欣赏。好了，下面就让我们欣赏一下九寨沟的美丽风光吧。

Han Jia: Daniel, don't you think these splashing water beads look like pearls?

Daniel: They do look like pearls bouncing in the sun. Hey, Han Jia, it reminds me of a verse I learned. "Big and small beads drop on the jade plate." It is perfect to describe the scenery here.

Han Jia: There is still much more to see at Jiuzhaigou. Will you become a poet after this trip?

Han Jia: There are still many more scenic spots at Jiuzhaigou. I guess you would become a poet after this trip.

Daniel: You think so? Then why don't we go quickly?

Han Jia: Take it easy. As we learn Chinese bit by bit, we should also enjoy the scenery bit by bit. Okay, let's enjoy the beautiful scenery of Jiuzhaigou now.

生词 Words and Expressions

1. 因…而…		yīn … ér …	therefore
2. 代表	（动）	dàibiǎo	to represent
3. 眼睛	（名）	yǎnjing	eye(s)
4. 保护	（动）	bǎohù	to protect
5. 环境	（名）	huánjìng	environment
6. 体现	（动）	tǐxiàn	to embody
7. 精神	（名）	jīngshén	spirit
8. 景色	（名）	jǐngsè	scenery
9. 欣赏	（动）	xīnshǎng	to enjoy

注释 Notes

1. **我们要像保护眼睛一样保护环境。**

   "像……一样"表示前后两种情况相似。

   "像…一样" means "to be/look like…", indicating the situations before and after "一样" are similar.

   例如：我们要像尊敬自己的父母一样尊敬老师。

2. **谁不想啊？**

   这是一个反问句，由有疑问代词的问句加上反问语气，这时句子已不表示疑问而表示反问。"谁不想"意思是"谁都想"、"每个人都想"。

   This is a rhetoric question in which the rhetorical mood is realized by a wh-question plus an interrogative intonation. "谁不想" means "everyone wants".

   例如：这件事谁不知道？

3. **一会儿你有的是机会。**

   "有的是"强调很多，不怕没有。

   "有的是" means "there is a lot", and one should have no fear of want.

例如：我们这儿能说流利汉语的人有的是。

4. 可以让它们自由的生长。

这是一个兼语句，"让"是动词，"它们"既是动词"让"的宾语，同时又是"自由地生长"的主语，"它们"这个词在句中兼有两种身份，所以称为兼语句，在兼语句中常用的动词有"请、叫、让"。

This is a pivotal sentence, in which "让" is the verb, while "它们" is both its object and the subject of "自由地生长". Such sentences are called pivotal sentences as "它们" has two grammatical functions. Besides "让", verbs such as "请，叫，让" are often used in pivotal sentences.

例如：你让我想一想。

他想请你吃饭。

我叫他去买东西。

5. 形容这儿的景色再合适不过。

某些形容词用在"再……不过"之间，表示所描写的程度最高。

Some adjectives placed between "再" and "不过" can be used as a superlative form of these adjectives.

例如：你能这样做，那是再好不过了。

6. 九寨沟里面的美景还多着呢。

助词"着呢"常与形容词连用，表示数量多、程度深，含有夸张意味，常用于口语。

The auxiliary expression "着呢" is used with an adjective, meaning large quantities, or great degrees and implying an exaggeration, often used in spoken Chinese.

例如：外面冷着呢，别出去了。

7. 你回去岂不成诗人了。

"岂"，副词，表示反问。"岂不成诗人了"意思是"变成诗人了"。

The adverb "岂" is used to construct a rhetorical question, and "岂不成诗人了" actually means "(You) have become a poet".

替换练习 Substitution Drills

1. 我们要像

保护	眼睛	一样	保护	环境。
对待	自己的亲人		对待	朋友
热爱	自己的生命		热爱	工作
关心	自己		关心	别人

2. 这里

处处	体现	环保	精神。
人人	喜欢	读书	看报
人人	关心	环境	卫生
处处	表现	民族	团结

3. 九寨沟

里面	的	美景	还多着呢。
好吃		东西	
好听		歌	
有意思		节目	

会话 Conversation

完成下列会话　Complete the following dialogues
（如括号里有词语或提示，请按要求做　Use words or phrases in the brackets）

A: 你们这儿有英文导游吗？

B: _____。（有的是）

A: 能帮我们请一个英文导游吗？

B: _____。

· ·

A: 明天早上我们到山上看日出，怎么样？

B: _____。

A: 有没有谁不想去？

B: _____?（谁）

九寨沟

【第二集】

韩　佳：大牛，你听说过一句话没有？"九寨归来不看水"。就是说，九寨沟的湖泊河流堪称一绝，很有看头。

大　牛：嗯，看头？什么意思？

韩　佳："很有看头"就是说，九寨沟的水非常美丽。

大　牛：可不是嘛。你看，这里的湖水被太阳这么一照，蓝蓝的，真像一个童话世界。

韩　佳：那一片叫芦苇海，在海拔2000多米高的地方还能长出那么茂盛的芦苇来，真是挺神奇的。①

大　牛：你看，还有从芦苇穿过去的水碧蓝碧蓝的，好像用颜料画出来的一样。

韩　佳：还有更神奇的呢，你看那边的山上，那块大岩石像不像一个姑娘的脸？

Nà kuài dà yán shí xiàng bú xiàng yì zhāng gūniang de liǎn?
那 块 大 岩石 像 不 像 一 张 姑娘 的 脸？

Does that cliff face look like a young girl's face?

韩　佳：那块大岩石像不像一个姑娘的脸？

大　牛：哎，真像！

韩　佳：哎，看出来了，行啊你！人家说一下子看出来的人能交好运。④

大　牛：那就太好了。

Han Jia: Daniel, have you ever heard of the saying "After returning from Jiuzhaigou, you won't enjoy seeing water elsewhere"? Which means the lakes and rivers at Jiuzhaigou are just marvelous and very beautiful.

Daniel: "Kantou"? What's the meaning?

Han Jia: "Hen you kantou" means the lakes and rivers at Jiuzhaigou are beautiful.

Daniel: Exactly. Look, the lakes here in the sun are really blue and look like a fairyland.

Han Jia: The area over there is called Reed Sea. At an altitude of over 2, 000 meters, it is really rare to see reeds growing so luxuriantly.

Daniel: Look, the water flowing through the reeds is so dark blue that it seems like an oil painting.

Han Jia: There is something more miraculous. Look at the mountain over there. Does the boulder look like a girl's face?

Daniel: Wow, it sure does!

Han Jia: Hey, you got it! Great. It is said those who could detect the likeness will have good luck.

Daniel: That's great.

火花海

大　牛：韩佳，这个湖亮闪闪的好像在冒火花一样。

韩　佳：所以，这儿就叫火花海。

大　牛：这个九寨沟真是个聚宝盆啊!

韩　佳：此话怎讲?

大　牛：你想，珍珠滩里有珍珠，火花海的湖水绿绿的像一大块翡翠，还有这些
　　　　火花像金银珠宝。

韩　佳：你比喻得还挺贴切。

大　牛：过奖了。②这里的湖水是那么清澈透明的。

韩　佳：这里的湖水都是那么清澈透明的，而且还有比湖水更好看的呢。③

Hái　yǒu　bǐ　húshuǐ　gēng　hǎokàn　de　ne.
还 有 比 湖水 更 好看 的 呢。

There are sights even better than these lakes.

卧龙海

大　牛：韩佳，这比湖水更好看的在哪呢?

韩　佳：别着急啊，你看那湖中间是不是有一条乳黄色的带子? 弯弯曲曲像一条
　　　　巨龙卧在水底。

大　牛：哎，你看，好像一条游龙。

韩　佳：这儿就叫卧龙海。

Daniel: Han Jia, this lake glitters with dazzling sparkles.

Han Jia: So it is called Sparkling Sea.

Daniel: Jiuzhaigou is a cornucopia indeed!

Han Jia: What do you mean?

Daniel: Just think. There are pearls on Pearl Beach. The Sparkling Sea is like a huge piece of jade. And these sparkles look like gold, silver and pearls.

Han Jia: It's an apt metaphor.

Daniel: I am flattered. The water of the lakes here is crystal and clear.

Han Jia: The lakes here are crystal clear. And there's something more beautiful than the lakes.

Daniel: Han Jia, where are those sights which are more beautiful than the lakes?

Han Jia: Take it easy. Look, isn't there an ivory yellow strip at the center of the lake? It looks like a huge dragon crouching at the bottom of the lake.

Daniel: Hey, look, the dragon is moving, looks swift swimming.

Han Jia: It is called Crouching Dragon Sea.

韩　佳：多美的镜子啊！⑤

大　牛：哦，女孩子就是爱照镜子。

韩　佳：我说的镜子在这儿呢。镜海这可不是一般的镜子，⑥里面有鱼在云中游，
　　　　鸟在水中飞的奇观。

大　牛：哇，这蓝天、白云、大山、绿树全在湖里，而且那么的清楚。这可是我
　　　　见过的最大的镜子。哎，韩佳，九寨沟的湖真多啊。

韩　佳：是啊，九寨沟大大小小的湖一共有 118 个呢。

大　牛：这么多啊？

韩　佳：大牛，既然我们来到了九寨沟就应该入乡随俗。

rù xiāng suí sú

入 乡 随 俗

When in Rome, do as Romans do.

韩　佳：知道"入乡随俗"的意思吗？

大　牛：当然知道了，这是我们英文的"when in Rome, do as the Romans do"的意
　　　　思。这里有什么样的风俗习惯呢？

韩　佳：当地人都管九寨沟的湖泊叫"海子"，⑦所以我们也别湖呀湖呀的了，应
　　　　该叫海子。

大　牛：海子，不错，这里的水蓝得像大海一样。

韩　佳：只可惜我们这次来的时间太短了，还有好多湖都没有介绍给大家呢。

大　牛：应该说这里还有好多海子没介绍给大家呢。刚教完我，她自己也忘了。

韩　佳：对，对，对，大牛老师教导得对，九寨沟的海子。好了，九寨归来不看
　　　　水，我们今天的节目就先到这里了。下面，我们再去领略一下九寨沟的美
　　　　景吧。

Han Jia: What a beautiful mirror!

Daniel: Well, girls like mirrors.

Han Jia: I mean the mirror here. Jing Hai (Mirror Sea) is not an ordinary mirror. It's one in which fish are swimming in cloudsand birds are flying water.

Daniel: Wow, blue skies, white clouds, big mountains and green trees all in the lake and they are also so clear. This is indeed the biggest mirror I've ever seen. Eh, Han Jia, there are so many lakes at Jiuzhaigou.

Han Jia: Yes. It has altogether 118 lakes of different sizes.

Daniel: So many!

Han Jia: Daniel, since we are at Jiuzhaigou, we'd better do as locals do.

Han Jia: Do you know what "ru xiang sui su" means?

Daniel: Of course. It's the same as "when in Rome, do as the Romans do" in English. What kind of customs do the locals have here?

Han Jia: Local people call a lake at Jiuzhaigou "haizi". So we'd better stop calling them lakes, and, instead, call them "haizi".

Daniel: Haizi is good. The water here is as blue as the sea.

Han Jia: What a pity we can stay here for only a short period of time! There are still many other lakes that we haven't introduced to you.

Daniel: We should say there are still many "haizi" that we haven't introduced to you. She just taught me the word, and now she forgot it herself.

Han Jia: Right. My teacher Daniel, you are right. Other "haizi" of Jiuzhaigou. All right. After returning from Jiuzhaigou, you won't enjoy seeing water elsewhere. That's all for our program today. Now, let's have some more glimpses of the beautiful scenery of Jiuzhaigou.

生词 Words and Expressions

1. 湖　　　　　（名）　hú　　　　　　　　lake
2. 神奇　　　　（形）　shénqí　　　　　　mysterious
3. 脸　　　　　（名）　liǎn　　　　　　　face
4. 镜子　　　　（名）　jìngzi　　　　　　mirror
5. 蓝　　　　　（名）　lán　　　　　　　blue
6. 入乡随俗　　　　　rù xiāng suí sú　　When in Rome, do as Romans do.
7. 介绍　　　　（动）　jièshào　　　　　to introduce

注释 Notes

1. 真是挺神奇的

"挺"这里是副词，用在形容词前，表示程度高，"很"的意思，常用于口语。

"挺" is an adverb here, used in front of an adjective, showing a high degree, meaning "very", "rather" or "quite" and often used in spoken Chinese.

例如：挺好　　　　挺不错　　　　挺高兴

2. 过奖了。

"过奖"是谦词，意思是过分地表扬或夸奖，常用于对方赞扬自己时。

"过奖" is an expression showing modesty, meaning "being flattered", and often used when one is being praised or commended.

例如：A: 你汉语说得真好。

　　　　B: 过奖了。

3. （这里）还有比湖水更好看的呢。

"比"这里是介词，常用句式为：A 比 B + 形容词

"比" is used as a preposition, and its pattern is: A 比 B + adj.

例如：今天比昨天冷。

4. 人家说一下子看出来的人能交好运。

这里"出来"用在动词后，表示事物随动作由隐蔽到显露。

Here "出来" is used after a verb, denoting something that appears from obscurity.

例如：那个男的我认出来了，他叫王大明。

5. 多美的镜子啊！

这里"多"是副词，"多么"的意思，常用在某些形容词前，表示程度高。

"多" is an adverb used before some adjectives, meaning "how..."or "what..." to imply a high degree.

例如：多好的天气啊！

6. 这可不是一般的镜子。

副词"可"常用来表示强调语气，多用于口语。

The adverb "可" is used for emphasis and is often used in spoken Chinese.

例如：山上的景点可好看啦。

7. 当地人都管九寨沟的湖泊叫海子。

用来称说人或事物，用于口语。

"管...叫..." is an expression to address people or things, used in spoken Chinese.

例如：他们管这种树叫神树。

替换练习 Substitution Drills

1. 那	块	大岩石	像不像	一	张	姑娘的脸？
	棵	树			把	伞
	座	山			匹	马
	块	石头			只	猴子

2. （这里）　　还有比　　湖水　　　更好看的呢。
　　 山上　　　　　　这里
　　 那里　　　　　　这个湖
　　 那边　　　　　　山下

3. 我们也得　　入乡随俗。
　　　　　　　学会几句藏语
　　　　　　　做些准备
　　　　　　　买些礼物

会话 Conversation

完成下列会话　Complete the following dialogues
（如括号里有词语或提示，请按要求做　Use words or phrases in the brackets）

A: 现在来这儿旅游的人多吗？

B: ＿＿＿＿＿＿＿＿＿＿＿＿。（挺）

A: 以前也这样多吗？

B: 不，＿＿＿＿＿＿＿＿＿＿。（比）

A: 这里的风景　　　　　　　（多＋形容词）

B: 是啊，这里水美山也美。

A: 你看，那座山＿＿＿＿＿＿＿＿？（像）

B: 挺像的。

九寨沟

【第三集】

场景 **原始森林入口**

韩　佳：大牛，咱们今天轻松一下，①我带你去补补氧。
大　牛：补氧？好啊。哎，九寨沟连氧吧都有啊。②
韩　佳：有啊，还是一个超大型的氧吧，而且还是免费的。
大　牛：啊？

场景 **原始森林**

韩　佳：大牛，别找了，就在这里。原始森林天然大氧吧。
大　牛：哎，早说嘛，那我得多吸几口。
韩　佳：九寨沟有两千多公顷的树林，新鲜空气让你吸个够。

Han Jia: Daniel, let's relax for a while today. I will take you to get some extra oxygen.

Daniel: Great. But is there an oxygen café at Jiuzhaigou?

Han Jia: Yes, and it is a super large one. And it is free.

Daniel: Wow.

Han Jia: Daniel, stop searching. It's right here. The primeval forest is a huge natural oxygen café.

Daniel: Hey, why didn't you say so earlier? I'd like to take a few more deep breaths here.

Han Jia: The forests at Jiuzhaigou cover an area of over 2, 000 hectares. So there is enough fresh air for you.

大　牛：三、四。

韩　佳：大牛，你在数什么呢？

大　牛：你看，这片湖它的颜色都不一样，我想数一数到底有多少种颜色。

韩　佳：这可难了，这个湖叫五花海。它的流水像孔雀开屏时候尾巴上的羽毛一样，五颜六色的，你数得过来吗？

大　牛：五颜六色，five colors and six shapes，那不就是一共有11种颜色吗？五颜六色。

韩　佳：不是，"五颜六色"是一个成语，形容颜色多种多样。

wǔ　yán　liù　sè
五　颜　六　色

colorful

韩　佳："五颜六色"是一个成语，形容颜色多种多样。湖水五颜六色。

大　牛：啊，我明白了，五颜六色就是颜色多种多样。这里的湖水五颜六色，我都看花眼了。③

韩　佳：那咱们就下去，走近点儿看看。

Daniel: Three, four.

Han Jia: Daniel, what are you counting?

Daniel: Look, there are various colors on the surface of the lake. I am counting how many colors there are.

Han Jia: It'd be difficult. The lake is called Wu Hua Hai (Five-Colored Sea). The water in it is like the colorful plumes of a peacock's fanned tail. How can you count the colors of a peacock tail?

Daniel: Five colors and six shapes… Would there be 11 in all? "Wu yan liu se".

Han Jia: It does not mean five colors and six shapes. It is an idiom meaning a variety of colors.

Han Jia: "Wu yan liu se" is an idiom meaning colorful or a variety of colors. The lake takes on a variety of colors.

Daniel: Oh, I see. It means colorful. "Wu yan liu se" means multicolored. The lake is so colorful that I feel dazzled.

Han Jia: Then, let's go down and take a closer look.

五花海

韩　佳：在这儿看五花海是最美的。
大　牛：嗯，这里的湖水也是五颜六色的。哎，你看，那像不像一条鳄鱼的大尖
　　　　嘴啊？
韩　佳：是啊，好像一条鳄鱼从水里探出脑袋来，栩栩如生啊。
大　牛：栩栩如生？
韩　佳："栩栩"是指生动活泼的样子。"栩栩如生"是一个成语，形容生动逼真，
　　　　像活的一样。水里的树枝像一条鳄鱼，栩栩如生。

xǔ xǔ　rú　shēng
栩 栩 如　生

striking realistic

场景 栈道

韩　佳：怎么样？九寨沟的景色很美吧？
大　牛：嗯，九寨沟的景色是很美。可是逛了老半天，④只是山啊、水啊、树啊，
　　　　没什么动物，无非只是一些像鳄鱼的树枝什么的。⑤
韩　佳：其实，九寨沟里面动物挺多的，飞禽走兽都有。只是游人一多就不容易
　　　　见到了。⑥但我起码能让你见到一种动物。
大　牛：真的？
韩　佳：Yea.
大　牛：女士优先，走。

Han Jia: It is a vantage point for seeing the Five-Colored Sea.

Daniel: Yes, the lake here is also colorful. Hey, does that look like a crocodile's snout?

Han Jia: Yes. It looks like a crocodile reaching out its head from the water. What a lifelike image!

Daniel: "Xuxu ru sheng"?

Han Jia: "Xuxu" means to be lifelike or vivid. "Xuxu ru sheng" is an idiom meaning to be like a real one lifelike. The reflection of a twig in the water looks like a real crocodile.

Han Jia: How's that? Isn't the scenery at Jiuzhaigou beautiful?

Daniel: Yes. The scenery at Jiuzhaigou is really beautiful. But after such a long time, we have seen so far just mountains, lakes and trees, but no animals. Just a few twigs with crocodile-shaped reflections in the water.

Han Jia: Actually, there are many animals at Jiuzhaigou, both birds and beasts. But it'd be difficult to see them due to the presence of so many humans here. But at least I can let you see one kind of animal.

Daniel: Really?

Han Jia: Yea.

Daniel: Ladies first. Please.

孔雀河道木桥上

韩 佳：大牛，你看那个黑色的鱼。那叫裸鲤，是九寨沟特有的。

大 牛：我看这种鱼个儿小，游得也快，挺有灵气的。

韩 佳：当地人都把它们当作是水中的精灵，而且从来不捕捉它们。

大 牛：那它们可真够幸福的，能够在这个美景里自由自在地生活。

Tāmen zài zhè lǐ zì yóu zì zài dì shēnghuó.
它们 在 这里 自由 自在 地 生活。

They live freely here.

大 牛：哎，韩佳，这九寨沟还有什么别的地方我们没玩儿呢？

韩 佳：九寨沟的美景多着呢，但是明天我们要换个花样，不再看美景了。

大 牛：九寨沟除了美景，还有别的好玩儿的事吗？⑦

韩 佳：当然有了。不过，今天我们的节目时间就已经到了。现在，再带大家去看一看九寨沟的美景。

Han Jia: Daniel, look at the black fish. It is called "luoli" carp peculiar to Jiuzhaigou.

Daniel: I find the fish to be small and fast in action. They are really cute.

Han Jia: Local people regard them as spirits in the water and never catch them for food.

Daniel: They are so lucky to be able to live a carefree life in this beautiful place.

Daniel: Hey, Han Jia, are there any other places that we haven't visited?

Han Jia: Jiuzhaigou has plenty of scenic attractions. But tomorrow, we will have something new to offer and won't see scenic spots anymore.

Daniel: In addition to scenic attractions, there are also fun places at Jiuzhaigou, right?

Han Jia: Of course. But it's time to wrap up today's program. Let's go and take one more look at the picturesque Jiuzhaigou.

生词 Words and Expressions

1.	氧	（名）	yǎng	oxygen
2.	森林	（名）	sēnlín	forest
3.	新鲜	（形）	xīnxiān	fresh
4.	空气	（名）	kōngqì	air
5.	颜色	（名）	yánsè	color
6.	数	（动）	shǔ	to count
7.	动物	（名）	dòngwù	animal
8.	除了…还…		chú le … hái …	besides, apart from...

注释 Notes

1. 咱们今天轻松一下……

"咱们"包括说话人和听话人双方，常用于口语，"我们"可以包括听话的人，也可以不包括听话的人。

"咱们" is a colloquial expression meaning "we", which may or may not include the listener.

例如：咱们现在就出发吧。

走吧，我们从这儿走，你们从那儿走。

2. 九寨沟连氧吧都有。

"连……都（也，还）……"这一结构常用来表示强调"连"后面的成份，可以是词，也可以是词组。

The structure "连... 都（也，还）..." is often used to emphasize what follows, which can be a word or a phrase.

例如：他连水都没喝就走了。

这件事连三岁的孩子都知道，你怎么会不知道？

3. 这里的湖水五颜六色，我都看花了眼。

"看花了眼"形容所看到的东西很多，已到了模糊分不清的地步。

"看花了眼" is used when one has seen so much that one's vision is blurred.

4. 逛了老半天

①这里"老"是副词，强调时间长。

Here "老" is an adverb stressing a long duration of the verb followed.

例如：他可能很忙，最近老没见到他了。

②这里"半天"指相当长的一段时间。

"半天" implies "for a long time".

例如：你上哪儿了，我等你半天了。

5. 无非只是一些像鳄鱼的树枝什么的。

"什么的"用在一个成分或并列的几个成分后，表示"等等"的意思，用于口语。

"什么的", a colloquial expression, is roughly an equivalent to "and so on" or "etc." in English. It is often used after one element or several parallel elements.

例如：星期六他就喜欢看电影什么的。

6. 游人一多就不容易见到。

"一……就……"表示前一种动作或情况出现后，紧接着发生另一种动作或情况，可以共用一个主语也可以分属两个主语。

"一 ... 就 ..." means the first action/event is the cause of the second or leads to the second immediately.

例如：他一忙就忘了吃饭。

每一次，我一说他就不高兴。

7. 九寨沟除了美景，还有别的好玩的事吗？

"除了……还（也）……"表示在什么之外还有别的。

"除了 ... 还（也）..." is equivalent to "besides", "apart from" or "in addition to".

例如：他除了会英语还会法语。

替换练习 Substitution Drills

1. 这里的湖水　　五颜六色。
　 这里的花
　 那些衣服
　 这些花布

2. 水里的树枝　　像　　一　　条　　鳄鱼，栩栩如生。
　 那座山　　　　　　　　　　匹　　马
　 那棵树　　　　　　　　　　个　　老人
　 山上那块石头　　　　　　　只　　猴子

3. 它们　　　　　　　在　这里　自由自在　地　生活。
　 他们　　　　　　　　　　　幸福
　 孩子们　　　　　　　　　　愉快
　 外国朋友们　　　　　　　　自由

会话 Conversation

完成下列会话　Complete the following dialogues
（如括号里有词语或提示，请按要求做　Use words or phrases in the brackets）

A: 这些花好看吗？
B: 好看，＿＿＿＿＿＿＿＿＿＿＿＿＿。（五颜六色）
A: 五颜六色是什么意思？
B: ＿＿＿＿＿＿＿＿＿＿＿＿＿＿。

· ·

A: 九寨沟的湖水真好看。
B: 太美了。
A: ＿＿＿＿＿＿＿＿＿＿＿＿＿＿。（除了…还…）
B: 当然有。

九寨沟

韩 佳：大牛，你在这儿干吗呢？找你半天了。

大 牛：嘘——别打扰我们了，我跟阚祝学藏语呢。

韩 佳：那你学会什么了？

大 牛：西泽吉。

韩 佳：什么意思啊？

大 牛：就是"你好"的意思。

韩 佳：啊，了不起，了不起。大牛都会说藏语了。

大 牛：可是，我只学会了一句。

大 牛：哎，韩佳，刚才去哪儿了？

韩 佳：你看，我找了一样好东西。

大 牛：手镯啊，真漂亮。在哪儿买的？

韩 佳：跟我来吧。哎，大牛，你看这绣花的小包，还有这图案，多精致啊！

大 牛：精致？

韩 佳：嗯，精致是一个形容词，形容非常的精巧细致。你看，这精致的图案。

Zhè tú'àn duō jīngzhì a !
这 图案 多 精致 啊！
This pattern is exquisite.

大 牛：哎，我知道了，英文是 exquisite。你看，这个帽子也挺精致的。嗯，藏帽头上戴，小伙子多帅。

Han Jia: Daniel, what are you doing here? I have been looking for you for a long time.

Daniel: Ah…Don't bother us. I am learning Tibeten with Kan Zhu.

Han Jia: What did you learn?

Daniel: ...

Han Jia: What does mean?

Daniel: That means "hello".

Han Jia: Wow, fabulous. Daniel can speak Tibetan.

Daniel: But I can only speak one sentence.

Daniel: Hey, Han Jia, where were you just now?

Han Jia: Look, I found something good.

Daniel: Bracelet, so beautiful. Where did you get it?

Han Jia: Follow me. Hey, Daniel, look at this embroidered purseand the exquisite design.

Daniel: "Jingzhi"?

Han Jia: Yes. "Jingzhi" is an adjective. It means exquisite. Look at the exquisite design.

Daniel: Hey, I know the English for it is exquisite. Look at the hat. It is exquisite too. Right. Tibetan hat. What a handsome guy with a hat!

九寨灵塔

大　牛：*这座白塔真精致啊！* 一、二、三、四、五、六、七、八、九。一共有九
　　　　座塔。

韩　佳：嗯，这叫九寨灵塔。这个是藏传佛教的建筑。这九座灵塔就代表了九个
　　　　村寨。

大　牛：啊，那旁边这高高迎风飘展的是什么？

韩　佳：哦，那是经幡。你看，上面还刻着经文呢。风一吹就表示念了一遍经。

大　牛：还有这样的说法？

韩　佳：嗯，你看，那边还有一个转经筒。

大　牛：哦，我刚到九寨沟不久，就已经发现了。

韩　佳：嗯，这里的灵塔、经幡、还有转经筒，都是表示祝福人们平安幸福的。

Zhù fú　·dà jiā　píng'ān　xìng fú.
祝福　大家　平安　幸福。
To wish everyone peace and happiness.

去藏族村寨的路上

大　牛：这九寨沟山美、水美、人也美，还这么有民族特色。

韩　佳：大牛，你这一路收获不小啊！

大　牛：嗯，收获不小，可是总觉得缺了点什么？①

韩　佳：大牛，我看你是饿了吧？

大　牛：这"民以食为天"嘛。走了这么多的路，咱们应该找一点儿好吃的慰劳
　　　　慰劳自己。

Daniel: This long white tower is really quite exquisite. There are 9 towers in total.

Han Jia: Right. They are called Jiuzhai Spirit Tower. It is a structure of Tibetan Buddhism. These nine spirit towers represent nine villages.

Daniel: Wow, what is that thing flying in the wind high up there?

Han Jia: Oh, it's prayer flag. Look, it has lection on it. Whenever the wind blows it, it means the heaven has just recited the lection once.

Daniel: There is such a story.

Han Jia: Look, there is a prayer wheel over there.

Daniel: Oh, I found it soon after I arrived at "Jiuzhaigou".

Han Jia: Right. The spirit towers, prayer flags and prayer wheelsall bless people with peace and happiness.

Daniel: Jiuzhaigou has beautiful mountains, lakes and people, and it has unique folk features.

Han Jia: Daniel, you have got a lot in the tour.

Daniel: Yes. A lot, but I always feel something missing.

Han Jia: Daniel, I bet you are hungry.

Daniel: Food is the first need of people. We have walked a long way. We should find something good to treat ourselves.

大　牛：好香！

韩　佳：别光顾着喝呀，②大牛。

大　牛：这"光顾着喝"是什么意思？

韩　佳：这个"光"是副词，是"只"的意思。我让你别光顾着喝，是想让你知道，这里面到底有什么？③

大　牛：好像有奶，还是麦子的香味。

韩　佳：真不错，你还真能喝出来。这是酥油茶。

大　牛："酥油茶"我知道，英文是 buttered tea。我还会唱呢。"不敬青稞酒，不打酥油茶，也不献哈达。"

韩　佳：行了，行了，对，这个是藏族的传统饮料。

Sū yóu chá　shì　Zàng zú　de　chuán tǒng　yǐn liào.

酥油茶　是　藏族的　传统　饮料。

Buttered tea is a traditional Tibetan drink.

韩　佳：这个是藏族的传统饮料。里面有糌粑和奶渣。这糌粑是由豌豆、青稞或者是燕麦做成的，④所以就有一股麦香味了。谢谢。

大　牛：酸酸的，还有一点甜。

韩　佳：嗯，这是青稞酒。

大　牛：嗯，我早就听说藏族的青稞酒很有名，俗称藏式啤酒。

韩　佳：没错。怎么样？今天我们教的内容您都记住了吗？

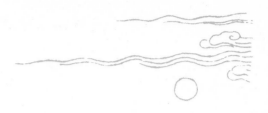

Daniel: So tasty.

Han Jia: Don't just drink, Daniel.

Daniel: What does "guang gu zhe he" mean?

Han Jia: "Guang" here is an adverb meaning just or only. I told you not to drink merely for the sake of drink but taste what is inside.

Daniel: Taste like milk and wheat.

Han Jia: Good, you got it. This is "Suyoucha".

Daniel: "Suyoucha". I know in English it is buttered tea. I can also sing. "No highland barley wine, no buttered tea, and no hada."

Han Jia: All right, all right. It is the traditional drink of Tibetans.

Han Jia: It has glutinous rice paste and milk. The glutinous rice paste is made of pea, highland barleyand oat. So it has a flavor of wheat. Thank you.

Daniel: A little bit sour and sweet.

Han Jia: Yes. It's highland barley wine.

Daniel: I have known long time ago that Tibetan highland barley wine is famous. It is also called Tibetan beer.

Han Jia: Exactly. Have you remembered what we learned today?

生词 Words and Expressions

1.	打扰	（动）	dǎrǎo	to trouble, to bother
2.	图案	（名）	tú'àn	pattern, design
3.	了不起	（形）	liǎobuqǐ	great, marveloous
4.	精致	（形）	jīngzhì	exquisite
5.	佛教	（名）	fójiào	Buddhism
6.	建筑	（名）	jiànzhù	building
7.	祝福	（动）	zhùfú	to wish someone good luck
8.	民族	（名）	mínzú	nationality, ethnic group
9.	特色	（名）	tèsè	special feature, characteristics
10.	传统	（名）	chuántǒng	tradition

注释 Notes

1. **可是总觉得缺了点什么。**

   这里"总"是副词，"一直"的意思。

   The adverb "总" is an adverb meaning "always".

   例如：他每天下午总要去锻炼身体。

2. **别光顾着喝呀。**

   这里"光"是副词，"只"的意思，"顾"是动词，"注意"的意思，常与"光"连用，意思是"只注意……"。

   "光"，an adverb meaning "only" and "顾" is a verb of action meaning "to be engaged in" or "to be concentrated on" which often appears together with "光"。"光顾"means "only pay attention to..." or "only be concentrated on..."。

   例如：他光顾着说话忘了去接电话。

3. **（我）是想让你知道这里面到底有什么？**

   "到底"这里是副词，常用于疑问句，表示进一步追究。

"到底" is an adverb usually used in interrogative sentences meaning "on earth".

例如：你到底想吃什么？

4. 这糌粑是由豌豆青稞或者是燕麦做成的。

"由……做成"表示一种东西是用什么来做的。

"由 ... 做成" is used to indicate what the subject is made of.

例如：豆腐是由大豆做成的。

5. 今天我们教的内容您都记住了吗？

动词"住"在这里补充说明"记"这一动作的结果，在汉语里，人们称它为结果补语，结果补语由动词和形容词充当，它的基本句式为：

The verb "住" is a complement to the result of the action "记". In Chinese, such verb is called complement of result. Adhectives can also be used as complement of result. The basic pattern is:

Subject + predicate verb + complement of result + object

主语	+	谓语动词	+	结果补语	+	宾语	
我		听		清楚			了。
他们		买		到		飞机票	了。

替换练习 Substitution Drills

1. 这图案　多　精致　啊！
　　衣服　　　漂亮
　　风景　　　好看
　　房子　　　有意思

2. 九寨沟地区　很有　民族　特色。
　　山下的别墅　　　中国
　　那些建筑　　　　西方
　　这些衣服　　　　东方

3. 酥油茶　　是　　藏族　的传统　饮料。
　　春节　　　中国　　　　　　节日
　　月饼　　　汉族　　　　　　食品
　　西服　　　西方　　　　　　服装

会话 Conversation

完成下列会话　Complete the following dialogues
（如括号里有词语或提示，请按要求做　Use words or phrases in the brackets）

A: 你到哪儿去了，我 _____ 。（半天）
B: 我去学藏语去了。
A: 学会了多少？
B: _____ 。（句）

• •

A: 你看，这帽子，怎么样？
B: _____ 。（特色）
A: 这图案多精致啊！
B: _____ 。（又…又…）

九寨沟

【第五集】

镜海旁

韩 佳、大 牛：哎，你们听！

高原黑：朋友们，大家好，我叫多吉。我叫阿日。我叫曲尔甲。我叫扎西拉。我叫
达尔基。欢迎大家来九寨。

韩 佳：呀，今天有新朋友加入。五个英俊的藏族小伙子。

合： 欢迎高原黑。

高原黑：大家好，今天我们一起去游览九寨沟。

大 牛：哎，还有什么好玩的地方我们没有去吗？

高原黑：还有一个最有名的地方你们还没去。

大 牛：是吗？

高原黑：是，跟我来。

诺日朗瀑布

韩 佳：大牛，你看，这比珍珠滩的瀑布还要大。

高原黑：这是诺日朗瀑布。是中国最宽的钙化瀑布。

大 牛：韩佳呀，在我们英语里我们管瀑布叫做 waterfall，就是"水落"的意思。
那么为什么中文会叫"瀑布"呢？

韩 佳：你看那一大片，从山地上面落下来的水像什么？

大 牛：我仔细琢磨琢磨，像一块挂着的白布。

韩 佳：嗯，真聪明。因为它像一块白布，所以我们叫它瀑布。[1]

Han Jia, Daniel: Listen, please!

Gaoyuanhei: Hello, friends! My name is Duoji. I'm Ari. I'm Qu'erjia. I'm Zhaxila. My name is Da'erji. You are welcome to Jiuzhaigou.

Han Jia: Oh, several new friends have come and joined us today. They are five handsome Tibetan young men.

All: Welcome you here.

Gaoyuanhei: Hello, everyone! Today we're going to tour Jiuzhaigou together.

Daniel: Well, are there any interesting places we haven't been to?

Gaoyuanhei: There is a well-known place you haven't been to.

Daniel: Really?

Gaoyuanhei: Yes. Please come with me.

Han Jia: Daniel,look! This waterfall is bigger than Zhenzhutan Waterfall.

Gaoyuanhei: This is Nuorilang Waterfall. It is the biggest travertine waterfall in China.

Daniel: Han Jia, the English for "pubu" is waterfall. It means the water falls down. Why in Chinese is it called "pubu"?

Han Jia: Look! What does the water look like, when it falls down the mountain?

Daniel: Let me think it over. It looks like a piece of hanging white cloth.

Han Jia: Yes. You're clever. Because it looks like a piece of white cloth, we call it "pubu" .

韩　佳：大牛，怎么样，发现什么了？

大　牛：你看，这树干都让水冲出坑来了。

韩　佳：这不应该叫"坑"，像这样两边高，中间凹下去的东西，凹下去那一部分叫做"槽"。

大　牛：树干被水冲出了一个"槽"。②

Shùgàn　bèi　shuǐ　chōng chū le　yí　gè　cáo.

树干　被　水　冲出了　一　个　槽。

The water has bored a trough in the tree trunk.

韩　佳：水滴石穿嘛，这穿了木头也不奇怪啊。

大　牛：哎，"水滴石穿"又是一个中国的成语？

韩　佳：没错，它的意思就是说，时间长了水滴都能把石头穿出洞来。现在比喻只要不懈地努力就一定会成功。③

大　牛：就像学中文。

韩　佳：哎，曲尔甲说要带我们去一个新鲜的地方。

高原黑：是啊，这可是九寨沟很有名的景点。

大　牛：那我们一起去看看吧。

高原黑：走。

Han Jia: Daniel, what did you see?

Daniel: Look! The trunk marks with pits made by water dripping.

Han Jia: It shouldn't be called "keng" (pit). The middle part is at a lower level than the edges of the both sides. The middle part is called groove.

Daniel: The groove was made on the trunk by water dripping.

Han Jia: The dripping water wears through rock. So it's not strange dripping water wears through wood.

Daniel: The dripping water wears through rock. Is that another Chinese idiom?

Han Jia: Yes. It means as time goes on, the dripping water can make a hole in a rock. It means constant effort will bring success.

Daniel: It is just like studying Chinese.

Han Jia: Well, Qu'erjia told me that he would take us to a new place.

Gaoyuanhei: Yes. It's a famous scenic spot in Jiuzhaigou.

Daniel: Then let's go and have a look.

Gaoyuanhei: Come on.

树正磨坊

高原黑：看，就这个。

大　牛：哎，这个小木屋是干什么用的？

韩　佳：哎，里边有个石磨，这小屋是个磨坊吧？

Zhè jiān xiǎo wū shì gè mòfáng.

这 间 小 屋 是 个 磨 坊。

This small room is a mill.

大　牛：啊，果然是个小磨坊。④

高原黑：嗯，这是从上面流下来的水，推动这个石磨转起来。

韩　佳：啊，是通过流水落差的自然力，这也算是一个微型的水利工程啦。

大　牛：它使我想起了荷兰的风车，只不过他们是用风作为动力的。

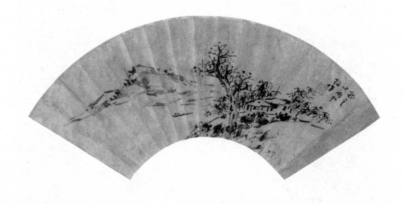

Gaoyuanhei: Look at this one.

Daniel: What's the use of this hut?

Han Jia: There is a millstone inside. This hut is used as a mill, isn't it?

Daniel: Oh, it's really a mill.

Gaoyuanhei: The water comes down and makes the millstone turn.

Han Jia: Oh! It utilizes a fall of the flowing water. Yes. It can be called a mini-water conservancy project.

Daniel: It reminds me of the windmills in Holland, except that they use wind as a source of power.

藏族民居

大　牛：这次九寨沟之旅真是不虚此行啊，⑤感觉这里像梦中的童话世界。

韩　佳：没错，不过这是你们西方人的说法。我们东方人一般都说这是人间仙境。

大　牛：嗨，反正不管怎么叫，就是说这里非常美。这里是人间仙境、童话世界。

高原黑：扎西德勒。

韩　佳：嗯，你瞧，哈达。哈达是藏族同胞心中的吉祥之物。

Hǎdá shì Zàng zú tóngbāo xīn zhōng de jíxiáng zhī wù.
哈 达 是 藏 族 同 胞 心 中 的 吉 祥 之 物。
A Hada is a lucky charm in the eyes of the Tibetans.

韩　佳：哈达是藏族同胞心中的吉祥之物。他们给我们献了哈达。怎么样，观众
　　　　朋友们，九寨沟的美景你看够了吗？到中国旅游，千万别忘了到童话世界
　　　　九寨沟。

Daniel: This is a worthwhile trip of Jiuzhaigou. It seems that it was the wonderland in my dream.

Han Jia: Yes. Wonderland is a term often used by you westerners. We usually call it fairyland on earth.

Daniel: Well, no matter what the name is, it all means this place is very beautiful like a fairyland or wonderland on earth.

Gaoyuanhei: Zha xi de le.

Han Jia: Look at this "hada". "Hada" is a mascot for the Tibetans.

Han Jia: "Hada" is a mascot for the Tibetans. They have presented Hada to us. Well, viewer friends, are you satisfied with all the beautiful scenes of Jiuzhaigou? When you come to China for a visit, be sure to come to visit this fairyland Jiuzhaigou.

生词 Words and Expressions

1. 游览　　（动）　　yóulǎn　　　go sight seeing
2. 好玩儿　（形）　　hǎowánr　　interesting, amusing
3. 只要　　（连）　　zhǐyào　　　if only
4. 成功　　（动）　　chénggōng　to succeed
5. 反正　　（副）　　fǎnzhèng　　anyway
6. 吉祥　　（形）　　jíxiáng　　　lucky
7. 千万　　（副）　　qiānwàn　　to be sure

注释 Notes

1. 因为**它像一块白布，**所以**我们叫它瀑布。**

　　这是一个因果复句，"因为"和"所以"都是连词，"因为"用在前一个分句，表示原因，"所以"用在后一个分句，表示结果。

　　"因为" and "所以" are both conjunctions. "因为" is used in the first clause, showing the cause while "所以" is used in the second clause showing the result.

　　例如：因为下大雨，所以我今天不去。

2. 树干被**水冲出了一个槽。**

　　在汉语里，表示被动意义的句子称为被动句，其中有一类句子在谓语动词前有一个介词"被（叫、让）"字，所以也称为"被"字句，其句式为：

　　This sentence is in the passive voice. In Chinese the passive voice can sometimes be realized by placing a preposition such as "被（叫，让）" before the predicate verb. Such sentences are called 被 -sentences. The pattern is:

主语　＋　介词"被（叫、让）"　　＋　宾语　＋　谓语　＋　其他成分
接受动作者　介词"被"　　　　　　　发出动作者　动词　表示完成或结果的词语
subject + prepositions "被（叫、让）" + objects + predicate + other elements
patient preposition　　　"被"　　　　　　　　doer　　　verb　　words indicating
　　　　　　　　　　　　　　　　　　　　　　　　　　　　　　　completion or result

房子　　　　　被　　　　　　大风　　刮　　　倒了。
词典　　　　　叫　　　　　　他弟弟　拿　　　走了。

3. 只要**不懈地努力**就**一定会成功**。

这是一个条件复句，连词"只要"指出所需要的条件，后一分句用副词"就"，引出结果。

This is a conditional complex sentence, in which "只要" points to the condition, while "就" leads to the result.

例如：只要你努力就一定能学好汉语。

4. **果然**是个小磨坊。

副词"果然"表示事实与所说的或所想的一致。

The adverb "果然" shows that the factual result is expected.

例如：他说这次比赛他想得第一名，果然得了冠军。

5. **这次九寨沟之旅真是**不虚此行**啊**。

这里"虚"意思是白白地、没有效果，"不虚此行"意思是这次到这儿来，很有收获，没有白来。

"虚" means "in vain" or "without result". "不虚此行" here means "it is worth the trip".

替换练习 Substitution Drills

1.	树干	被	水	冲出了	一	个	槽。
	房子		人	砸坏了		扇	门
	衣服		人	撕破了		个	洞
	石头上		水	冲出了		道	沟

2. **这间小屋是个** 磨坊。

　　　　　　书房

　　　　　　卧室

　　　　　　客厅

3. 哈达　　　　　是　　　　藏族同胞心中　　　　　的吉祥之物。
　　猴子　　　　　　　　　峨眉山
　　熊猫　　　　　　　　　今年全国运动会
　　这个图案　　　　　　　这次展览会

会话 Conversation

完成下列会话　Complete the following dialogues
（如括号里有词语或提示，请按要求做　Use words or phrases in the brackets）

A: 这里为什么叫九寨沟？

B: _____。（因为）

A: 这次来九寨沟旅游不错吧。

B: _____。（不虚此行）

・・・・・・・・・・・・・・・・・・・・・・・・・・・・・

A: 树干上这个槽是叫水冲出来的吗？

B: 没错，_____。（让）

A: 这让我想起了一个中国成语。

B: 哪个成语？

A: _____。

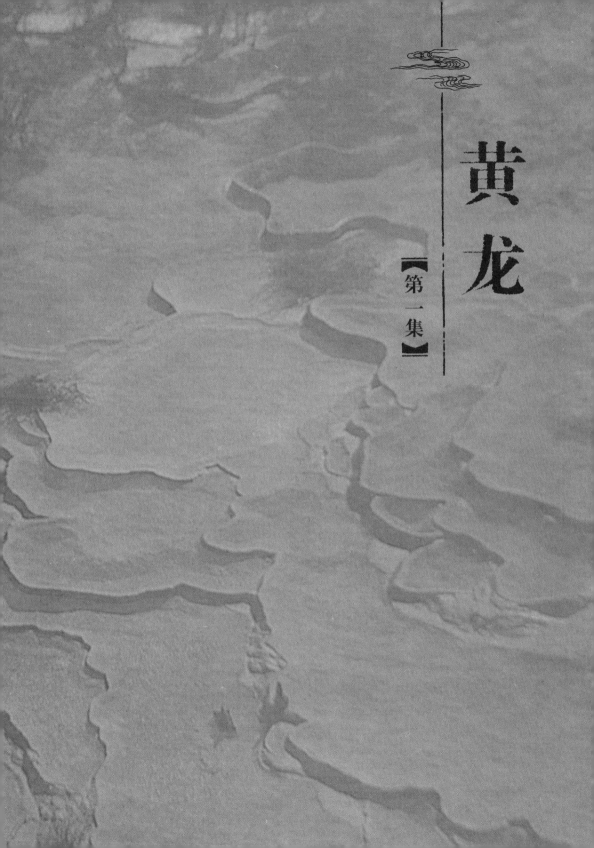

黄龙

【第一集】

韩　佳：今天啊，我们带您到著名黄龙牟尼沟去学习汉语。

大　牛：我听说黄龙牟尼沟的景色很迷人哪。

韩　佳：黄龙牟尼沟啊，最吸引人的就是它的颜色。

Huánglóng　zuì　xīyǐn　rén　de　shì　tā　de　yánsè.

黄 龙 最 吸 引 人 的 是 它 的 颜色。

The most attractive aspect of Huanglong is its many colors.

韩　佳：那咱们的黄龙牟尼沟之旅就以颜色为线索吧。①

大　牛：哎，韩佳，你知道这个机场口出口在哪儿吗？

韩　佳：在那吧，你是不是冷了？

大　牛：嗯。快点！

韩　佳：谢谢。

一西木初：我叫一西木初，很高兴你们到我的家乡黄龙。

大　牛：哇，你看，雪山哪！

一西木初：对，那就是著名的雪宝顶。

韩　佳：雪宝顶是岷山山脉的顶峰，海拔有 5588 米呢。就因为它高，所以峰顶的白雪长年不化。

大　牛：要是谁以后跟我提黄龙，我第一反应，肯定是这片纯净的白色。

韩　佳：你先别那么早下结论，另一种颜色，同样可以占据你整个视野。

Han Jia: Today we're going to take you to the well-known place Munigou at Huanglong and to learn Chinese there.

Daniel: I was told that the scene of Munigou at Huanglong is very charming.

Han Jia: The most attractive scene of Munigou is its color.

Han Jia: Then our trip of Munigou will follow the color.

Daniel: Hi, do you know where is the exit of the airport, Han Jia?

Han Jia: It's over there, isn't it? Do you feel cold?

Daniel: Yes. Be quick!

Han Jia: Thank you.

Yiximuchu: My name is Yiximuchu. I'm very glad to meet you here in my hometown.

Daniel: Oh, look at the snow-capped mountain!

Yiximuchu: That is the well-known Xuebaoding.

Han Jia: Xuebaoding is the highest peak in Mount Min range. It's 5,588 meters above sea level. Because of the height, the mountaintop is covered with snow all the year round.

Daniel: If someone mentions Huanglong later on, what first occurs to me will surely be this pure white color.

Han Jia: Don't jump to conclusions now. Another color can also be within your field of vision.

韩 佳：第二种颜色就是灿烂的黄色。这里是黄龙最具代表性的景观之一，②金沙铺地。

大 牛：这么大一片沙子。

韩 佳：哎，这可不是沙子啊。

大 牛：哎，等等。韩佳，你刚才在这里说了，"这可不是什么沙子"。

韩 佳：对。

大 牛：这句话里面的"可"是什么意思？

韩 佳："可"在这里是副词，用来强调语气，常用于口语当中。举个例子吧："我可不知道。""你可得说到做到。"

大 牛：我可不知道。你可得说到做到。

韩 佳：金黄色啊是黄龙的地质特点。

Zhè   zhǒng   jīn huáng sè   shì   Huánglóng   de   dì zhì   tè diǎn.

这　种　金黄色　是　黄龙　的　地质　特点。

This kind of golden color is a geological trait specific to Huanglong.

Han Jia: The color is bight yellow. This is one of the most typical scenic spots here in Huanglong. The land is covered with golden sand.

Daniel: There is so vast expanse of sand here.

Han Jia: "Zhe ke bushi shazi" (This is not sand).

Daniel: Well, no hurry. Han Jia, just now you said "zhe ke bushi shenme shazi" .

Han Jia: Yes.

Daniel: What does the word "ke" mean in this sentence?

Han Jia: "Ke" is an adverb, used to stress the mood. It's often used in spoken Chinese. Here is an example. "I have got no idea." "You must stick to your word. "

Daniel: I have got no idea. You must stick to your word.

Han Jia: This golden yellow is the geological feature of Huanglong.

莲台飞瀑

韩 佳：看！这就是黄龙的龙爪了。

大 牛：哎，真像，难怪叫黄龙。

韩 佳：对，这里是黄龙的三个世界之最其中的一个，①世界上最大的地表钙
华滩流。

大 牛：哎，韩佳刚才你说它是三个世界之最其中的一个。嗯，那另外两个呢？

一西木初：一个是世界上最大的钙华塌陷壁——洗身洞。 一个是世界上最大的露
天钙华彩池群——争艳池。

62

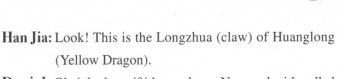

Han Jia: Look! This is the Longzhua (claw) of Huanglong (Yellow Dragon).

Daniel: Oh, it looks as if it's a real one. No wonder it's called Huanglong.

Han Jia: Yes. Here in Huanglong, this is one of the three bests of the world. It is the biggest travertine surface beachland.

Daniel: Han Jia, just now you said it is one of the three bests of the world. Yes. How about the other two bests?

Yiximuchu: One is the biggest travertine collapse wall – Xishen (Body Washing) Grotto. The third one is the biggest travertine pond – Zhengyan Pond.

大　牛：一西木初，这儿的水池修得很特别啊，大小形状都不一样啊。

一西木初：我们可修不出这么漂亮的水池啊。

韩　佳：哈哈，大牛。你说的这些整齐的像人工砌起来的池壁呀，其实都是大自然的杰作。

大　牛：不会吧?

韩　佳：真的是天然的。这是由于长期的钙华沉积和水流的冲刷而形成的。④大自然的杰作更胜于能工巧匠。⑤

大　牛：嗯。今天我可真是大开眼界。

韩　佳：嗯。

Jīntiān　wǒ kě shì dà kāi yǎn jiè a.
今天　我 可 是 大 开 眼 界 啊。

I really broadened my horizons today.

大　牛：啊，我明白了，黄龙嘛，它当然是以灿烂的黄色为主。要是以后谁跟我提黄龙的事呢……

韩　佳：你就说黄色最具有代表性了，是吗?

大　牛：对。

韩　佳：告诉你吧，还有好多颜色你还没见着呢。

大　牛：还有?

韩　佳：嗯。不过观众朋友们，今天我们节目结束的时间又快到了。⑥没关系，我们来轻松一下。看一看黄龙美丽的景色。

Daniel: Yiximuchu, the ponds here are very unique. They vary in size and shape.

Yiximuchu: We can't build such beautiful ponds.

Han Jia: Oh, Daniel. These neat pond walls that look as if they were built by man were actually made by nature.

Daniel: I don't think so.

Han Jia: It's really natural. It results from long-time travertine deposit and water washing. The masterpiece of nature is better than that of the skillful craftsman.

Daniel: Yes. Today what I've seen really helps broaden my horizon.

Han Jia: Yes.

Daniel: Oh, I see. The main color of Huanglong is certainly the bright yellow. If someone mentions Huanglong later on …

Daniel: You'll tell him the yellow color is the most typical of Huanglong, won't you?

Daniel: Yes.

Han Jia: I'll tell you the truth. There are many other colors you haven't seen yet.

Daniel: Are there?

Han Jia: Yes. Well, viewer friends, now we are going to conclude our program. All right. Let's relax for a while. Let's have a look at the beautiful scenes of Huanglong.

生词 Words and Expressions

1. 迷人　　（形）　　mírén　　charming
2. 吸引　　（动）　　xīyǐn　　to attract
3. …之一　　　　　…zhī yī　　one of ...
4. 以…为…　　　　　yǐ … wéi …　　with... as...
5. 特点　　（名）　　tèdiǎn　　characteristics
6. 难怪　　（副）　　nánguài　　no wonder
7. 其中　　（名）　　qízhōng　　among, within
8. 大自然　　（名）　　dàzìrán　　nature
9. 大开眼界　　　　dà kāi yǎn jiè　　broaden one's vision

注释 Notes

1. 咱们的黄龙牟尼沟之旅就以颜色为线索吧。

   "以……为……"这一结构，它的意思是"把……作为……"。

   The structure "以... 为..." means "with...serving as...".

   例如：明天后天这里的天气以晴为主，大家可以出去活动活动。

2. 这里是黄龙最具代表性的景观之一。

   "……之一"意思是"其中的一个"。

   "...之一" means "one of ...".

   例如：长城是中国的名胜古迹之一。

3. 这里是黄龙的三个世界之最其中的一个。

   "最"是副词，表示极端，胜过其余。"之最"意思是"最……"

   "最"，an adverb, is used to show the highest degree. "之最" means "最 ...".

   例如：他有两个全校之最，一个是身高最高，一个是年龄最小。

4. 这是由于长期的钙华沉积和水流的冲刷而形成的。

这里"而"是个连词，它把前面表示原因的成分连接到动词上。

"而" is a conjuction roughly equivalent to "as a result" in English which introduces the reason for the action after "而".

例如：这次航班由于天气不好而晚了两个小时才起飞。

5. 大自然的杰作更胜于能工巧匠。

这里"于"是介词，用在形容词后表示比较，用于书面。

"于", a preposition, is used after an adjective to show comparison in written Chinese.

例如：由于大家的努力，今年我们的成绩要好于去年。

6. 我们节目结束的时间又快到了。

汉语里，用"要……了"、"就要……了"、"快……了"、"快要……了"表示动作或情况很快就要发生或出现。

Expressions such as "要...了", "就要...了", "快...了", "快要...了" mean some action or event is going to happen in no time.

例如： 飞机要起飞了。

飞机就要起飞了。

飞机快起飞了。

飞机快要起飞了。

句中有时间状语不能用"快要……了"、"快……了"。

However, when there is adverbial of time in the sentence, the structures "快要...了", "快 ... 了" cannot be used.

替换练习 Substitution Drills

1. 黄龙	最	最吸引人的是它的	颜色。
长城			历史
九寨沟			自然环境
黄山			黄山松

2. 这种　　金黄色　　是　　黄龙　　的　　地质　　特点。
　　　　　设计　　　　　　　　这里　　　　建筑
　　　　　衣服　　　　　　　　那地方　　　民族
　　　　　打扮　　　　　　　　那里　　　　地方

3. 今天我可是　　大开眼界　啊！
　　　　　　　　大饱口福
　　　　　　　　大长见识
　　　　　　　　大吃一惊

会话 Conversation

完成下列会话　Complete the following dialogues
（如括号里有词语或提示，请按要求做　Use words or phrases in the brackets）

A: 今天看完这几个景点，感觉怎么样？

B: ＿＿＿＿＿＿＿＿＿＿＿＿＿＿＿。（大开眼界）

A: 这里最吸引你的是什么？

B: ＿＿＿＿＿＿＿＿＿＿。（吸引）

A: 这个景点怎么样？

B: 听说＿＿＿＿＿＿＿＿。（…之一）

A: 那我们应该好好儿地看一看。

B: 没错。

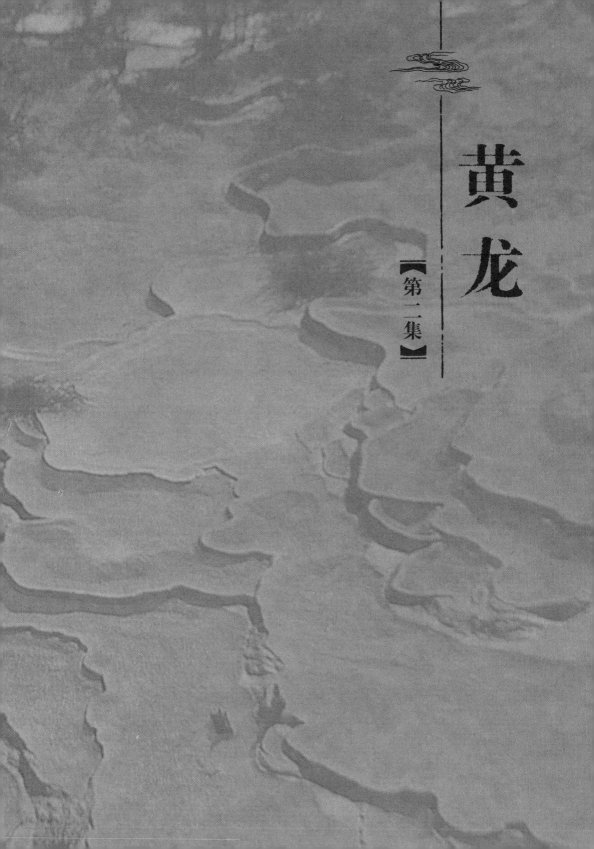

黄龙

【第二集】

黄龙古寺

大　牛：哎，韩佳，昨天你夸下海口，①说要带我去看其他颜色的美景。

韩　佳：嗯。

大　牛：今天你可不能说话不算数啊。②

韩　佳：当然不会了。我们说走就走。③我啊，这就带你去看看棕色色调的景色去。

Wǒ   zhè   jiù   dài   nǐ   kànkan   zōng sè   sè diào   de   jǐng sè   qù.
我　这　就　带　你　看看　棕色　色调　的　景色　去。

Now I'll take you to see some scenery of a brownish hue.

Daniel: Hi, Han Jia. Yesterday you boasted that you could take me to the scenic
spots with other colors.

Han Jia: Yes.

Daniel: You should mean what you said.

Han Jia: Sure. Let's go right now. Now I'll take you to see the scenes with brownish
hue.

韩 佳：大牛，你看那匾。

大 牛：韩佳，那个匾哪是棕色的？④是蓝色的呀。

韩 佳：别着急嘛，你念念它那的几个字。

大 牛：黄龙古寺。

韩 佳：然后你再到右面去念念。

大 牛：奇怪。

韩 佳：大牛，你看!

大 牛：哦，这倒是棕色。⑤嗯，可是那上面那字？

韩 佳：是什么？

大 牛：飞阁流丹。

韩 佳：聪明。咱们再到左边去看看。

大 牛：哇，怎么又变了？居然是山空水碧。如果不是亲眼所见，很难让人相信。

Rúguǒ .bú shì qīnyǎn suǒ jiàn, hěn nán ràng rén xiāngxìn.

如果 不 是 亲眼 所见，很 难 让 人 相信。

If I haven't seen it with my own eyes, I'd find it hard to believe.

Han Jia: Daniel, look at that inscribed board there.

Daniel: Han Jia, how should you say that board is brownish? It's bluish.

Han Jia: Take your time. Just read those characters.

Daniel: "Huanglong Gu Si" (Huanglong Old Temple).

Han Jia: Then you'll go and stand on the right side and read it.

Daniel: It's strange.

Han Jia: Daniel, look at it!

Daniel: It is brownish. But what are the characters on it?

Han Jia: What?

Daniel: "Fei ge liu dan".

Han Jia: Yes. Let's go to the left side and have a look.

Daniel: Oh, it is different. It turns out to be "shan kong shui bi." If you haven't seen it with your own eyes, you can hardly believe it.

韩 佳：我们现在要去看的这第二个景啊，可跟你有点关系啊。

大 牛：啊，也是棕色的吗？

韩 佳：嗯，黄龙有棕色的，牟尼沟也有啊。

大 牛：还跟我有关系？

韩 佳：对。

大 牛：哎，我知道了。嗯，我到这里的第一天，就有个人跟我说，牟尼沟有一
　　　 个地方叫犀牛鼻。要我一定去看看。

韩 佳：对了。我们现在要去看的正是犀牛鼻。⑥大牛就是大牛！

大 牛：当然了，都占一个牛字嘛。

Han Jia: Now the second scene we are going to visit has something to do with you.

Daniel: Is it also brownish?

Han Jia: Huanglong has brownish hues and so does Munigou.

Daniel: Does it have something to do with me?

Han Jia: Yes.

Daniel: Oh, I see. On the first day when I just came here, someone told me that, there is a scenic spot namely Xiniu Bi (rhinoceros nose) at Munigou. He asked me to go there and have a look.

Han Jia: All right. Now we are going to visit Xiniu Bi. Da Niu is so great!

Daniel: Of course. There is the word Niu both in Da Niu and Xiniu Bi.

犀牛鼻

韩 佳：这是犀牛鼻，像不像一个牛鼻子啊？

大 牛：哎，特别像。你看里面还有清鼻涕。啊。不，说错了，泉水。

韩 佳：有意思吧。

大 牛：挺有意思的。哎，他们在干嘛呢？

韩 佳：他们是一对恋人。

Tāmen shì yí duì liànren .

他们 是 一 对 恋人。

They are a pair of lovers .

韩 佳：他们是一对恋人。

大 牛：哎，这个对是量词吧？

韩 佳：对在这里就是量词。可以说一对恋人，一对夫妻。有时候还可以用于正
反事物，比如说一对矛盾。

大 牛：哦，我明白了。"对"是一个中文的量词，好比英文中的"pair"。比如
说：一对恋人。

韩 佳：哎，大牛，这个犀牛鼻还有一个很有意思的说法呢。哦。一对恋人或是
一对夫妇把他们各自的手都伸到这个鼻孔里面去，然后呢，如果在水底
下，他们如果能够互相握着的话，他们就会有美满的姻缘。

大 牛：啊。原来挖犀牛的鼻子也很浪漫呀。

恋 人：还没呢。

大 牛：加油啊。

韩 佳：哎，你们握着了吗？

恋 人：握着了，握着了。

大 牛：恭喜你们！祝你们白头偕老！

韩 佳：永结同心！

Han Jia: This is Xiniu Bi. Does it look like rhinoceros nose?

Daniel: It's really like it. Look at it! There is nasal mucus. Oh. No, it's not. It's spring water.

Han Jia: It's funny.

Daniel: Yes. What are they doing?

Han Jia: They are a pair of lovers .

Han Jia: They are a pair of lovers .

Daniel: Here the word "dui" is a measure word, isn't it?

Han Jia: Yes. It's a measure word here. We may say "yi dui lianren", "yi dui fuqi" (husband and wife). Sometimes "Yi dui" can be used to express the two opposite things. "yi dui maodun" (contradiction).

Daniel: Oh, I'm clear. "Dui" is a Chinese measure word that is used as our English "pair". For example, a pair of lovers.

Han Jia: Da Niu, there is a saying about this nose. It's very funny. If a couple or young lovers put their hands into the nostril respectively, and in the water if they can hold their hands they will have the happy marriage, together.

Daniel: Oh. So picking rhinoceroses' nose is also very romantic.

Han Jia: Well, have you held hands?

Lovers: Not yet.

Daniel: Come on.

Lovers: Yes, come on.

Daniel: Congratulations. May you live together to a ripe old age.

Han Jia: And love each other forever.

韩　佳：我们今天节目虽然要结束了，但是还是要带大家去欣赏一下黄龙牟尼沟
　　　　美丽的景色。

大　牛：当然，怎么会忘呢？

韩　佳：哎。观众朋友们，咱们可约好了，明天要带您去看更多颜色的景色，到
　　　　那时候大牛更该吃惊了。

Han Jia: Before we end our today's program, we are going to take you to have a look at the beautiful scenes at Munigou of Huanglong.

Daniel: Of course, how could I forget?

Han Jia: Viewer friends, I can make sure that tomorrow I'll take you to see the scenes with more colors. At that time Daniel will be more pleasantly surprised.

生词 Words and Expressions

1. 棕色　（名）　　zōngsè　　　　　　brown
2. 色调　（名）　　sèdiào　　　　　　tone
3. 亲眼　（副）　　qīnyǎn　　　　　　in one's own eyes
4. 相信　（动）　　xiāng xìn　　　　　to believe
5. 恋人　（名）　　liànren　　　　　　lover
6. 鼻子　（名）　　bízi　　　　　　　nose
7. 关系　（名）　　guānxi　　　　　　relation
8. 美满　（形）　　měimǎn　　　　　　happy

注释 Notes

1. **昨天你夸下海口。**

　　漫无边际地说大话称为"夸海口"。这里"下"表示"夸"这个动作已完成。

"夸海口" means "bragging or exaggerating", while "下" denotes the action has been completed.

　　例如：别听他在那儿夸海口了。

2. **今天你可不能说话不算数啊。**

　　承认说出去的话有效力称为"算数"。

"算数" means "what one says counts".

　　例如：我说话是算数的，明天我一定来参加你们的活动。

3. **我们说走就走。**

　　"动词 + 就 + 动词"这一结构表示"就"前后两个动作紧接着发生。

The pattern "verb + 就 + verb" expresses the two actions occur one after another.

　　例如：你看，那个孩子说哭就哭了。

4. **那个圖哪是棕色的？**

　　这里"哪"用于反问，表示否定，也可以换成"哪儿"，意思是"那个圖不是棕色的"。

"哪" used in rhetoric questions to express negation. When "哪儿" is used, the speaker negates the other's statement."哪" can be replaced by "哪儿" here.

例如：我不相信，哪有这样的事？

5. 这**倒**是棕色。

这里"倒"是副词，表示出乎意料。

The adverb "倒" is used to express unexpectedness.

例如：真有这样的事？我倒要听听。

6. 我们现在要去看的**正**是犀牛鼻。

这里"正"是副词，加强肯定的语气。

The adverb "正" is used for affirmative emphasis.

例如：正因为下雨，我们才不能出去参观。

替换练习 Substitution Drills

1. 我这就带你看看　棕色色调的景色　去。
　　　　　　　　　那山上的寺庙
　　　　　　　　　原始森林
　　　　　　　　　这里的建筑

2. 如果不是　　亲眼所见，很难让人相信。
　　　　　　我自己来
　　　　　　他告诉我
　　　　　　我妈妈说的

3. 他们是一　对　恋人。
　　　　　　对　夫妻
　　　　　　批　学生
　　　　　　群　运动员

会话 Conversation

完成下列会话　Complete the following dialogues
（如括号里有词语或提示，请按要求做　Use words or phrases in the brackets）

A: _____。（算数）

B: 当然。

A: 那我们现在就走吧。

B: 好，咱们_____。（动词＋就＋动词）

• •

A: 那毛衣是蓝色的吗？

B: _____？　（哪）

A: _____？　（颜色）

B: 那是绿色的。

黄龙

【第三集】

植物

韩 佳：今天我们要去看一看，黄龙美丽的自然生态环境。黄龙是一个天然植物资源宝库。这里有1500多种高等植物呢。

Zhè li yǒu yī qiān wǔbǎi duō zhǒng gāoděng zhíwù.
这里 有 一千 五百 多 种 高等 植物。
There are over 1500 different kinds of higher plants located here.

黄龙森林内

大 牛：哎，我现这里的树都是垂直的。

韩 佳：教你一个词吧，"笔直"。树干啊是笔直的。

大 牛：我记住了。①你看看我们的周围，我们现在就走进了一个绿色的世界。

韩 佳：嗯，你看这儿。

大 牛：哦，这不是moss吗？苔藓。

韩 佳：对，这就是苔藓，又叫地衣。

大 牛：不叫第二。

韩 佳：地衣对空气的检测能力，可是人类的1000倍呢。空气中只要有一点儿不好的气体，它们就会消失的，可是你看这儿几乎随处都可以看到地衣。

大 牛：说明这里的空气好，没有污染。

韩 佳：没错。

Zhè li de kōng qì hǎo, méi yǒu wūrǎn.
这里 的 空气 好，没有 污染。
The air here is great, completely without pollution.

Han Jia: Today we're going to pay a visit to Huanglong, the beautiful natural ecological environment. Huanglong is a natural treasure-house of plants. There are more than 1500 species of higher plants here.

Daniel: I've noticed that the trees here are all "chuizhi" (vertical).

Han Jia: I'll tell you a word "bizhi" (upright). The trunk is upright.

Daniel: I've learned it by heart. Now look around. We are now in the green world.

Han Jia: Look at here.

Daniel: Is it moss?

Daniel: Moss.

Han Jia: Moss? Yes. It's moss. It's called "diyi".

Daniel: Not "di'er".

Han Jia: Its capability to test air is 1000 times as much as the human capability. If there is a little bad gas in the air, the moss will die. But here you can see it everywhere.

Daniel: It shows the air is fresh, without any air pollution.

Han Jia: Yes.

韩 佳：黄龙的绿色之所以这么的吸引人，②全应了中国的一句老话：天时地利人和。③

大 牛：哎，韩佳，你说的这个天时地利，我自己都能体会，但是说到人和，我就不知道你指的是什么了。

韩 佳：我的意思是说，自然环境再好，也需要人们的爱惜和保护，④而黄龙的居民，正是给了这片绿色最大的关爱。

大 牛：我明白了。这里的人们非常爱护他们身边的环境。毫无疑问，这里生长着很多植物。

韩 佳：不仅这里的人喜爱保护这片风景，这里的绿色还吸引了一位像你一样的热爱这片土地的外国朋友呢。

大 牛：真的吗？

韩 佳：他在这里工作了好几年，而且还娶了一位中国新娘呢。

大 牛：哎，刚才你说了，他在这里工作了好几年。这里面的"好"是什么意思啊？

韩 佳："好"在这里是副词，常用在"多"或"几"前面，用来强调"多"或者"久"。

大 牛：哦，我明白了。"好"，在这里是副词，经常用在"几"或者"多"前面表示强调。就是说他在这里工作了好几年了。那他是谁呢？

韩 佳：他就是德国生态学家，豪格尔·帕奈。

Han Jia: That the green Huanglong attracts people so much results from, as the saying goes, its favorable climatic, geographical and human conditions.

Daniel: Han Jia, I can see the favorable climatic and geographical conditions myself. But what do you mean by the human conditions?

Han Jia: I mean that no matter how nice the natural environment is, it's still necessary for people to cherish and protect it. People here in Huanglong cherish very much this green environment.

Daniel: I know that people here cherish the environment very much. It's no wonder that there are so many kinds of plants are growing here.

Han Jia: People here protect the scenery. The green scene has also attracted a foreign friend who loves this land as you do.

Daniel: Really?

Han Jia: He has been working here for several years and married a Chinese girl.

Daniel: Just now you said "Ta zai zheli gongzuo le hao ji nian". What does the word "hao" mean here?

Han Jia: "Hao" is an adverb, often used before "duo" or "ji" . It's used to stress "duo" or "jiu" .

Daniel: Oh, I see. third tone, is use here as an adverb. It can be used in front of words like "ji" or "duo" to add emphasis. He has been working here for several years. Who is he?

Han Jia: He is a German ecologist, Holger Perner.

大　牛：你好！

豪格尔：你们好！

韩　佳：我们是快乐中国栏目的主持人。

豪格尔：（德语）

韩　佳：听说豪格尔先生为黄龙培育了很多的高山花卉，真佩服您。

大　牛：真羡慕您，能够在这么美丽的地方工作生活。

豪格尔：（德语）

大　牛：嗯，他说能在这里生活工作，他感觉很幸运。

Néng zài zhè li shēnghuó gōngzuò, wǒ juéde hěn xìngyùn.

能 在 这里 生活 工作，我 觉得 很 幸运。

I feel very lucky to be able to live and work here.

大　牛：他说能在这里生活工作，他感觉很幸运。因为我们是到美丽的黄龙才认识的，我来教您一句汉语，⑤好不好？

豪格尔：好。

大　牛：我爱黄龙。

豪格尔：我爱黄龙。

大　牛：哎，对。

韩　佳：好了，观众朋友，我们今天节目结束的时间又快到了。后面还有黄龙好风光，等着你欣赏呢。

Daniel: Hello!

Holger: Hello!

Han Jia: We are anchorpersons of Happy China.

Holger: (German)

Han Jia: It's said that you has cultivated many kinds of alpine flowers. I really admire you.

Daniel: I really envy you for you can work and live in such a beautiful place.

Holger: (German)

Daniel: He said that he was lucky to work and live here.

Holger: He said that he was lucky to live and work here. After we come to this beautiful we've got to know each other. Huanglong, Shall I teach you a Chinese sentence?

Holger: Ok.

Daniel: I love Huanglong.

Holger: I love Huanglong.

Daniel: Yes.

Han Jia: Viewer friends, it's time for us to conclude our program. There are more beautiful scenes of Huanglong worth your seeing.

生词 Words and Expressions

1.	植物	（名）	zhíwù	plant
2.	绿色	（名）	lǜsè	green
3.	污染	（名）	wūrǎn	pollution
4.	热爱	（动）	rè'ài	to love
5.	佩服	（动）	pèifú	to admire
6.	觉得	（动）	juéde	to feel, to think
7.	幸运	（形）	xìngyùn	fortunate

注释 Notes

1. **黄龙的绿色之所以这么吸引人，全应了中国的一句老话。**

   "……之所以……"用在表示因果关系语句中说明结果。

   "...之所以..." is used to express the result of a cause-effect sentence.

   例如：我之所以考这个大学是因为这个大学很有名。

2. **天时、地利、人和。**

   "天时"指适宜的气候条件；"地利"指优越的地理环境；"人和"指人们团结、认识一致。总的意思是要做成一件大事，既要有有利的客观条件又要有人们的积极性。

   "天时" refers to favorable weather conditions; "地利" geographical environment and "人和" means unity and concensus. This sentence means that both favorable objective conditions and people's enthusiasm are needed to accomplish great deeds.

3. **自然环境再好，也需要人们的爱惜和保护。**

   副词"再"这里表示一种让步的假设，含有"无论怎么"的意思，后面常有"也"呼应。

   The adverb "再" expresses a suggestion in concession, implying "however..." with "也" to correspond to it afterward.

   例如：你再去向他解释他也不会同意。

4. 我来教你一句汉语。

这是一个连动句，同时又是一个双宾语句。

谓语由两个或两个以上连用的动词或动词词组组成的句子称为连动句，两个动词或动词词组共用一个主语。

This is a verbal construction in series and a double object sentence as well. Sentences with predicate made up of two or more consecutive verbs or verbal phrases are called verbal constructive in series. In such constructions, the two verbs or verbal phrases share the same subject.

例如：中国人用筷子吃饭。

有些连动句的第一个动词用"来"，这"来"不表示实在的"来"的意思，只表示一种意愿，有缓和语气的作用。

The first verb "来" in some verb construction in series does not mean "come", rather, it means intention.

例如：我来介绍一下儿这儿的情况。

汉语里有些句子，谓语动词所涉及的宾语有两个，一个是人，一个是事物，指人的称为间接宾语，指事物的做为直接宾语，间接宾语在直接宾语之前。

Like English, Chinese verbs sometimes take two objects, direct and indirect.

例如：张老师教我们汉语。

替换练习 Substitution Drills

1. 这里	有	一千五百多	种	高等植物。
那湖里		二百多		鱼类
这山上		一百多		动物
那里		三十多		花儿

2. 这里的	空气	好，没有污染。
	环境	
	河水	
	卫生	

3. 能在这里生活、工作，我觉得很幸运。
   见到你们
   为你们服务
   为你们当导游

会话 Conversation

完成下列会话　Complete the following dialogues
（如括号里有词语或提示，请按要求做　Use words or phrases in the brackets）

A: 你为什么要来黄龙旅游？
B: _____。（…之所以…）
A: 你们来了几个人？
B: _____。（好）

· ·

A: 这儿的纪念品很便宜，你买了吗？
B: 没有，_____。（再…也…）
A: 为什么？
B: 我的东西太多了。

黄龙

【第四集】

大　牛：哎，韩佳，今天你要带我去看什么颜色，蓝色或者紫色？

韩　佳：你应该问蓝色"还是"紫色？因为"或者"和"还是"在英文里面都翻译成or，但是在中文里面，疑问句里面就要用"还是"，陈述句里面就应该用"或者"。

大　牛：哦，我明白了。"还是"用在提问当中，"或者"用在陈述句当中。韩佳呀，今天我们要去看什么颜色呢？

韩　佳：今天我们要去看的是黄龙和牟尼沟的水。

大　牛：哦，水呀！嗯，水是透明的没有颜色。

韩　佳：可是就是因为它透明，才可以折射出各种各样的颜色，所以说，我们今天看到的颜色是五彩缤纷的。

大　牛：五彩缤纷？嗯，这就是颜色很多的意思吧？

韩　佳：对。五彩缤纷的水。

Daniel: Han Jia, what color will you take me to see, blue or purple?

Han Jia: You should have said blue "haishi" purple. Because "huozhe" and "haishi" both can be translated into "or" in English. But in a Chinese interrogative sentence, "haishi" should be used while in a declarative sentence, "huozhe" should be used.

Daniel: Oh, "haishi" is used in the questions but "huozhe" is used in statements. Han Jia, what color are we going to see?

Han Jia: We're going to see the water of Huanglong and Munigou.

Daniel: Oh, water! The water is transparent and has no color.

Han Jia: Just because of its transparency, it can refract light and you can see many colors. So what we have seen today will be blazing with colors.

Daniel: "Wu cai binfen". Yes. It means there is a riot of color, isn't there?

Han Jia: Yes. The colorful water.

扎嘎瀑布

韩 佳：哎，大牛。我们先来看看牟尼沟磅礴的水吧。这个可是世界上第一钙华瀑布，叫扎嘎瀑布。那个瀑布有104米，而且它下落的速度是每秒钟23米，可想而知它的气势了吧。

素花湖

韩 佳：大牛，这儿就是素花湖了。素花湖是牟尼沟最美的湖泊之一。

Sùhuā Hú shì Mù ní gōu zuì měi de húpō zhī yī
素花 湖是 牟尼沟 最 美 的 湖泊 之 一。

Suhua Lake is one of the most beautiful lakes in Munigou .

韩 佳：这里到了开花的季节，在湖里面会开出无数的小花来，而且这些小花都是一种颜色的，还会形成一个一个的花环，所以才叫素花湖。

大 牛：哦，我明白了。到时候，这里就会变成花的海洋。

Han Jia: Da Niu, let's first go and see the majestic water of Munigou. It's the first travertine waterfall in the world. It's called Zhage Waterfall. It is 104 meters long. And its fall rate is 23 meters per second. So you can imagine how powerful it is.

Han Jia: Da Niu, this is Suhua Lake. Suhua Lake is one of the most beautiful lakes in Munigou.

Han Jia: When in the season with flowers in bloom, there will be countless little flowers on the lake. And all these flowers are in one colour and form garlands one after another. So it's called Suhua Lake (Light-Colored Flower Lake).

Daniel: Oh, I see. When the time comes, it will become an ocean of flowers.

韩 佳：哎，上面两处牟尼沟的水或壮观或秀气，①可是都只有一种颜色。最后我
　　　们要去的这个地方——

大 牛：就是真正的五彩缤纷。

韩 佳：哎，大牛，你可以啊。居然一下子把这处美景的名字都说出来了。

大 牛：我说什么了？

韩 佳：你刚才说的那个就是下一处美景的名字——五彩池。

大 牛：五彩池？

Han Jia: The water of Munigou above is either majestic or graceful. But both are in · one colour. Yes. The last place we're going to visit is −

Daniel: really blazing with colors.

Han Jia: Oh, how great you are, Daniel! You can even tell us the name of this scenic spot.

Daniel: What did I say?

Han Jia: What you said is just the name of the next scenic spot, Wucai chi (Multi-colored Ponds)

Daniel: Wucai Chi?

场景 五彩池

韩 佳：大牛，你看那就是黄龙著名的五彩池了。

大 牛：果然是五彩缤纷啊！你看每个池子里边的水的颜色，都是不一样的。

韩 佳：是啊，恐怕连画家都不能说出这些颜色的具体名字来。②

大 牛：哎，那边是什么？

韩 佳：哦，那个呀，那个是古代一位将领的陵墓。五彩池的池壁每年都会上涨一厘米。慢慢地这个陵墓就被淹没了。③

大 牛：是吗？那你快帮我在这里拍张照片吧。

Nǐ kuài bāng wǒ zài zhè li pāi zhāng zhàopiàn ba.
你 快 帮 我 在 这 里 拍 张 照 片 吧。

Quick! Help me take a photo here.

大 牛：你快帮我在这里拍张照片吧。

韩 佳：好。

大 牛：几年之内，他们就将完全消失了。

Han Jia: Da Niu, look! This is the well-known Wucai Chi of Huanglong.

Daniel: It is multi-coloured indeed. Look at the water in each of the ponds. They are different in color.

Han Jia: Yes. I'm afraid even the artist can hardly tell these colors' name.

Daniel: Well, what's that over there?

Han Jia: What is that? That is the tomb of a general of the ancient time. The walls of Wucai Chi increase by one centimeter each year. Gradually this tomb will be buried in the water.

Daniel: Well, then help me take a photo here, please.

Daniel: Please help me take a photo here.

Han Jia: All right.

Daniel: In the few years, they will all disappered.

五彩池

韩　佳：相传啊，王母娘娘想把五彩池带到天上去欣赏。④善良的达美姑娘辛苦地把这座五彩池留在了人间。可是她特别地累，以至于忍不住就睡着了。

大　牛：五彩池连天上的神仙都要抢，看来，这里的景色比天宫还要美。

Zhè lǐ de jǐng sè bǐ tiān gōng hái yào měi.

这里的景色比天宫还要美。

The scenery here is even more beautiful than that of the kingdom of heaven.

韩　佳：五彩池啊，被称作是黄龙的眼睛。我们到最后来欣赏这儿的美景，也可以说是画龙点睛⑤了。观众朋友们，明天我们要去牟尼沟，来一回奇妙的马帮旅行。哎，大牛，别忘了戴上你的牛仔帽。

大　牛：没问题。

Han Jia: Tradition has it that Queen Mother of the Western Heavens wanted to take Wucai Chi to heaven for her own enjoyment. But Damei, a kind-hearted girl, tried her best to keep Wucai Chi on earth. Because she was very tired and soon fell asleep.

Daniel: Since the god in heaven wanted to get Wucai Chi, you can see the scenery here is more beautiful than that of heaven.

Han Jia: Wucai Chi is called the eyes of Huanglong (yellow dragon). Since we come here to see this beautiful scenery at our last stop, we can say it is really to bring the painted dragon to life by putting in the pupils of its eyes. Viewer friends, tomorrow we're going to ride on a horse to tour Munigou. Daniel, don't forget to bring your cowboy hat with you.

Daniel: Sure.

生词 Words and Expressions

1. 或者　　　　（连）　　huòzhě　　　　　　or else
2. 还是　　　　（连）　　háishi　　　　　　 still; yet
3. 明白　　　　（动）　　míngbai　　　　　　to understand
4. 各种各样　　　　　　　gè zhǒng gè yàng　various
5. 五彩缤纷　　　　　　　wǔ cǎi bīnfēn　　 colorful
6. 速度　　　　（名）　　sùdù　　　　　　　 speed
7. 恐怕　　　　（副）　　kǒngpà　　　　　　 perhaps, probably
8. 拍照片　　　　　　　　pāi zhàopiàn　　　to take photos

注释 Notes

1. **上面两处牟泥沟的水或壮观或秀气。**

　　"或……或……"这一结构表示几种交替的情况，意思是"有的……有的……"

　　The pattern "或 ... 或 ..." means "ome...others..." expressing there exists several alternative situations.

　　例如：每天下午操场上都有很多人锻炼，或打球或跑步。

2. **恐怕连画家都不能说出这些颜色的具体名字来。**

　　"连…都…"请参看本书第三课。

　　For the expression "连…都…" please refer to Lesson Three of the book.

3. **这个陵墓就被淹没了。**

　　在汉语的被动句里，有一类句子"被"后的宾语（动作的施动者）有时可以省略，基本句式为：

　　In a Chinese passive sentence, the object to "被"(by) can sometimes be omitted, and its basic pattern is:

主语　　+　介词"被"　　+　谓语　+　其他成分

Subject + preposition "被" + predicate　+ other elements

陵墓　　　被　　　　　淹　了。

窗户　　　被　　　　　吹　开了。

有关"被"字句，请参看本书第5课。

For 被 -structure, please refer to Lesson Five of the book.

4. **皇母娘娘想把五彩池带到天上去欣赏。**

在"把"字句里，助动词或否定副词要放在介词"把"之前。

In the 把 -structure, auxiliary verbs or negative words should be placed before "把".

例如：星期三以前你能把书看完吗？

昨天晚上他没把信写完就睡觉了。

5. **画龙点睛**

　　这是一个成语。传说一千多年前，中国有个画家在一个寺庙墙壁上画了四条龙，不点眼睛。他说如果点了眼睛，龙就会飞走。听的人不相信，一定要他点上，他刚点了两条，两条龙就飞走了。现在常用来比喻作文、说话或做事时，在关键地方加上精辟的东西，使整个内容更加生动传神。

　　"画龙点睛" is an idiom. As the legend goes, a thousand years ago, there was a painter who painted four dragons without eyes on the wall of a temple. He said the dragons would fly away if he did. Others would not believe him and insisted that he should add eyes to the dragons. As soon as he finished adding eyes to two of the dragons, the two flew away immediately. This idiom is now used to mean that once something incisive is added to the key points of something, say a written article or speech or a painting, the whole thing will be more vivid.

替换练习 Substitution Drills

1. 素花湖	是	最	美丽	的	湖泊	之一。
长江			著名		河流	
黄山			有名		旅游胜地	
这些房子			古老		建筑	

2. 你快帮我在这里   拍张   照片   吧。
                      找个   导游
                      买些   礼物
                      订张   机票

3. 这里的景色   比   天宫   还要   美。
   这些景点   那些景点   好看
   这里的人   那里的人   热情
   这种纪念品   那种纪念品   便宜

会话 Conversation

完成下列会话   Complete the following dialogues
（如括号里有词语或提示，请按要求做   Use words or phrases in the brackets）

A: 你每天都要看报纸吗?

B: 对，我每天都要看报纸。

A: 看什么报纸?

B: _____。（或…或…）

A: 风很大，你去看看门关好了没有?

B: 门 _____。（被）

A: _____。（把）

B: 好，我把门关上了。

黄龙

牟尼沟的村寨

大　牛：哎，你看我这身打扮怎么样？

韩　佳：嗯，还真有点儿马帮骑士的劲头，不过不知道你骑马的技术怎么样了。

大　牛：我骑马的技术啊，那还用说，当然不怎么样了。①

韩　佳：难得今天大牛也谦虚起来了。

大　牛：其实我骑马的技术还是不错的。

Wǒ qí mǎ de jì shù hái shi bú cuò de .
我 骑 马 的 技术 还是 不错 的。

My equestrian skills aren't bad.

大　牛：其实我骑马的技术还是不错的。可是我来到这里之后，就看到了那些马
帮的小伙子、姑娘们的骑术，我就一点自信也没有了。

韩　佳：别没自信啊！咱们正好趁这个机会，跟他们好好学习学习。

Daniel: How do you think of my clothes?

Han Jia: Well, you really look like a rider. But I want to know how is your horsemanship.

Daniel: My horsemanship? Tell you the truth, it's not so good.

Han Jia: It's really great of Daniel to be so modest today.

Daniel: Actually my horsemanship is not bad.

Daniel: Actually my horsemanship is not bad. But after I come here and have seen the the girls and boys, horsemanship of I have no confidence in myself now.

Han Jia: Don't lose your confidence! Let's take this chance to learn from them.

场景 牟尼沟的小路上

韩　佳：马帮旅游是牟尼沟最具特色的生态旅游项目之一。

大　牛：嗯，只要是来过这里，无论是中国人还是外国人都会在"Happy trails"的带领下经历一番特别的马背之旅。②

韩　佳：嗯，"Happy Trails"是快乐小路的意思。是松潘马帮给自己取的名字。

大　牛：他们叫快乐小路，我们是快乐中国，都是快乐的，所以我们今天就来一次快乐中国快乐游吧。

韩　佳：说得好，那我们赶快行动吧！

大　牛：驾！

韩　佳：大牛，行啊你！　进步得够快的。

大　牛：对啊，连师傅都夸我聪明。

韩　佳：是啊。你还真行啊，不过咱们也别光顾着玩了，得抓紧时间，③我们今天晚上得自己亲手搭帐篷，要不然只能露宿在外边了。

大　牛：搭帐篷？嗯，露营我最拿手了，④你就看我的吧。

Han Jia: To ride on horseback and to tour Munigou is one of the typical ecotourism programs here.

Daniel: Yes. No matter who comes here, a Chinese or a foreigner, he will be taken to have a special trip on horseback.

Han Jia: It means a happy trail. It is the name given by themselves to their own team.

Daniel: They are given the name Happy Trail. This is Happy China. We are all happy. So let's make a happy tour in China.

Han Jia: Great! Let's go quickly!

Daniel: Go!

Han Jia: How great you are, Daniel! You're making rapid progress.

Daniel: Yes. Even my teacher has praised me for my horsemanship.

Han Jia: Yes. You are really great. But we can't only play. We must be quick to pitch tents for ourselves. Otherwise during the night we have to camp in the open air.

Daniel: To pitch a tent? Yes. I'm sure I can do the job well. You can count on me.

韩　佳：瞧！这是 tent，帐篷。晚上大家都要住在自己搭的帐篷里。

Wǎnshang dà jiā dōu yào zhù zài zì jǐ dā de zhàngpeng li .
晚上　大家都要住在自己搭的帐篷里。

In the evening, everyone has to live in the tent which they pitched by themselves.

韩　佳：大牛正在搭帐篷，⑤可是他搭帐篷的水平好像不怎么高。大牛，搭得怎么样了？

大　牛：别急嘛，这回肯定没错。

韩　佳：可是你都说三回了。⑥太阳就要下山了，天都快黑了。

大　牛：好了，好了。你看这不就已经搭起来了吗？快进去试试。

韩　佳：大牛，这行吗？

大　牛：当然行了。进去。快点!

韩　佳：哎呀，哎呀。

大　牛：对不起。

韩　佳：大牛，你不是说行了吗？

大　牛：对不起，对不起。哎，韩佳，坐在自己亲手搭起来的帐篷前感觉就是好。

韩　佳：是不是觉得比五星级酒店还要好啊？

Wǒ juéde zhè li bǐ wǔ xīng jí jiǔ diàn hái yào hǎo .
我　觉得这里比五星级酒店还要好。

I think that here is even better than a five star hotel.

别　人：篝火晚会快开始了。

韩　佳：啊，哎，有篝火晚会。咱们去换一身漂亮的衣服吧。

大　牛：哎，有青稞酒喝，还有烤肉吃呢。嗯，来。

Han Jia: Look! This is a tent. We'll spend the night in the tents pitched by ourselves.

Han Jia: Daniel is pitching a tent. But it seems that he is not good at doing the job. Daniel, how is it?

Daniel: No hurry. This time I think it's OK.

Han Jia: But you've said it three times. The sun is setting. It's getting dark.

Daniel: All right. Look! Is it OK now? Just go inside and have a look.

Han Jia: Is it all right, Daniel?

Daniel: Sure. Come in. Be quick!

Han Jia: Oh .

Daniel: I'm sorry.

Han Jia: Did you say it's OK now?

Daniel: I'm terribly sorry. Han Jia, I feel good sitting before the tent pitched by myself.

Han Jia: Don't you think it's even better than the five-star hotel.

Others: A campfire party will begin soon.

Han Jia: Oh, there will be a campfire party. Let's go and put on the beautiful clothes.

Daniel: There will be qingke barley beer and barbecue. Please come here.

别　人：这是我们藏族的青稞家酒。

大　牛：谢谢，谢谢，我干了啊!

韩　佳：上面是凉的，下面是热的，味道不错啊!

大　牛：就是青稞酒啊。

韩　佳：哎，观众朋友们，你是不是也被这儿的热闹气氛所吸引了呢? 黄龙牟尼
沟山美水美，而且这儿地藏族朋友们又更加地热情好客，一定要来黄龙牟
尼沟来看一看啊。

Bieren: This is our Tibetan qingke barley beer.

Daniel: Thank you very much. Cheers!

Han Jia: The upper part is cool and the lower part is warm. It tastes good.

Daniel: Qingke barley beer.

Han Jia: Viewer friends, are you also inspired by the joyous atmosphere here? There are beautiful mountains and rivers at Munigou of Huanglong. Besides, the Tibetans here are known for their hospitality. Be sure to come and pay a visit to Munigou of Huanglong.

生词 Words and Expressions

1.	骑	（动）	qí	to mount
2.	技术	（名）	jìshù	techneque, technology, skill
3.	机会	（名）	jīhuì	opportunity, chance
4.	夸	（动）	kuā	to exaggerate, to praise
5.	亲手	（副）	qīnshǒu	in person
6.	帐篷	（名）	zhàngpéng	tent
7.	感觉	（动）	gǎnjué	to feel
8.	晚会	（名）	wǎnhuì	evening party

注释 Notes

1. 不怎么样

"不怎么样"意思是平平常常，不很好。

The expression "不怎么样" means "just so so", or "not very good".

例如：我觉得那个景点不怎么样，我不喜欢。

2. 无论是中国人还是外国人都会……经历一番特别的马背之旅。

"无论……还是……"这一结构表示不受所说条件的影响。

In this case, the expression "无论 ... 还是 ..." means "either" or..." in English.

例如：无论是冬天还是夏天，这儿的气候都很宜人。

3. 咱们也别光顾着玩啊，得抓紧时间。

"得"这儿是助动词，读"děi"，表示情理上或事实上的需要，"应该"、"必须"的意思。

"得" is an auxiliary verb here and is pronounced as "děi", meaning "have to" in English. Here "得" indicates a need thay is reasonable and factual.

例如：时间不早了，你得快一点儿。

4. 露营我最拿手了。

对某种技艺很擅长，称为拿手。

The expression "拿手" means "very good at doing something".

例如：唱京剧他很拿手。

5. 大牛正在搭帐篷。

汉语里，副词"正在"加动词可以表示动作正在进行，基本句式如下：

The adverb "正在" followed by a verb in Chinese is used to express an action or an event is going on. The pattern is:

主语　　+ 正在 + 动词 + 宾语

subject + 正在 + verb + object.

他　　　　正在　　吃　　饭。

6. 你都说三回了。

这里副词"都"意思是"已经"的意思。

"都" means "已经", an equivalent to "already".

例如：都十二点了，快睡觉吧。

替换练习 Substitution Drills

1. 我　骑马　的技术还是不错的。
　　　做饭
　　　打球
　　　开车

2. 晚上大家都要住在　自己搭的帐篷　里。
　　　　　　　　　　山上的酒店
　　　　　　　　　　新建的别墅
　　　　　　　　　　藏族同胞家

117

3. 我觉得这里比　　五星级酒店　　　　还要好。
　　　　　　　　　　昨天住的酒店
　　　　　　　　　　山下的别墅
　　　　　　　　　　自己家里

会话 Conversation

完成下列会话　Complete the following dialogues
（如括号里有词语或提示，请按要求做　Use words or phrases in the brackets）

A: 这儿每天的游客都这么多吗?

B: _____。（无论…还是…）

A: 四点多了，你们几点下班?

B: 五点, _____。（快要…了）

• •

A: 这个景点怎么样?

B: _____。（太…了）

A: 刚才那个景点呢?

B: 我不太喜欢。

峨眉山

【第一集】

"天下名山" 石前

大　牛：今天，我们到的是天下名山——

韩　佳：峨眉山，世界自然文化遗产之一。

> Éméi　Shān　shì　Shìjiè　Zìrán　Wénhuà　Yíchǎn　zhī　yī.
> **峨 眉 山 是 世界 自然 文化 遗产 之 一。**
> Mount Emei belongs to our World Naural Cultural Heritage.

震旦第一山

大　牛：*震旦第一山*。哎，韩佳，看来这座山不一般哪。

韩　佳：那当然了。哎，大牛，你再看看这边。

大　牛：哦，什么一山？

韩　佳：那是震旦第一山。

大　牛：哎，*什么叫"震旦"？*

韩　佳："震旦"是指太阳升起的地方，这是古印度人对中国的称谓。

大　牛：那你倒是说说峨眉山有哪些奇妙的景观可以称得上是名山甚至第一山呢？[①]

韩　佳：峨眉山的美景谁都知道啊。

> Éméi　Shān　de　měijǐng　shuí　dōu　zhīdào.
> **峨 眉 山 的 美景 谁 都 知道。**
> Everyone konws of Mt Emei's beautiful scenery.

韩　佳：峨眉山的美景谁都知道啊。首先就是峨眉山的四大奇观。

大　牛：哪四大奇观呢？

韩　佳：日出、云海、佛光、圣灯。

大　牛：哦！

Daniel: Today we've come to Mt. Emei.

Han Jia: One of the famous mountains in the world. It belongs to the world natural and cultural heritage.

Daniel: The No. 1 Mountain under the sun. Hi, Han Jia, The mountain looks unusual.

Han Jia: Yes. Daniel, look at this on this side.

Daniel: What is it?

Han Jia: It's "Zhendan Di Yi Shan" (The First Mountain in Zhendan).

Daniel: What does "Zhendan" mean?

Han Jia: "Zhendan" means the place where the sun rises. This was what the ancient Indians called China.

Daniel: Then please tell us which of the fantastic scenic spots in Mt. Emei can be called the famous mountains or the first mountain?

Han Jia: The beautiful landscape of Mt. Emei is well known to all.

Han Jia: The beautiful landscape of Mt. Emei is well known to all. The four Wonders of Mt. Emei rank first.

Daniel: What are the four Wonders?

Han Jia: They are sunrise, the sea of clouds, Buddha's halo and the holy lamp.

Daniel: Oh!

场景 峨眉山下

大　牛：咱们赶紧去看奇观吧。先从第一奇观看起，一个一个看。②

韩　佳：你看看都几点了？

大　牛：哎，在这里"都几点"是什么意思？

韩　佳："都"在这里是已经的意思。

大　牛：哦，我明白了。"都"在这里是一声，有"已经"的意思。比如，已经三点了。

韩　佳：这个时候看日出晚了点吧？

大　牛：也是。

韩　佳：再说了，要看峨眉的四大奇观啊，必须要先爬上海拔3079米的金顶。

大　牛：啊，那么高啊！

场景 金顶

韩　佳：终于爬上来了。大牛，这儿就是金顶了。金顶是峨眉山奇景最多的地方了。

大　牛：这里好冷啊！③

韩　佳：冷吧？宋代的苏东坡有诗说："春风日日吹不消，五月行人冻如蚁。"不过我们有办法，瞧，这儿有棉衣，赶快穿上吧。

大　牛：哎，谢谢啊。暖和多了。

韩　佳：哎！你看那边有轻轨观光车。我们去那儿看云海吧。

大　牛：好啊。

Daniel: Let's go and have a look at these Wonders. We'll start from the first Wonder and see them one by one.

Han Jia: Could you tell me what's the time now?

Daniel: What does the term "dou ji dian" mean?

Han Jia: The word "dou" means "already".

Daniel: Oh, I see. "Dou" here first tone, means already. For example, it's already three o'clock.

Han Jia: Is it a bit late for us to watch the sunrise at this time?

Daniel: Yes, it is.

Han Jia: Besides, if you want to see the four Wonders of Mt. Emei, first, you have to climb onto the golden top that is 3079 meters above sea level.

Daniel: Ah, it's so high.

Han Jia: At last we've made it. Daniel , here is the golden top. Standing on the golden top, you can see most of the Wonders.

Daniel: It's so cold.

Han Jia: Are you cold? There are two verses of a poem written by Su Dongpo, a poet of the Song Dynasty: "Although spring breeze day in day out, people are still shivering with cold in May". But I can deal with it. Look! Here are some cotton-padded clothes. Be quick to put it on.

Daniel: Thank you very much. This is much warmer.

Han Jia: Look! There are light-rail sightseeing trains over there. Shall we go to watch the sea of clouds there?

Daniel: All right.

大　牛：这里真是太美了，像仙境一样。

Zhèli zhēn shì tài měi le, xiàng xiānjìng yí yàng.
这里　真　是　太　美　了，像　仙境　一样。

It's so beautiful here, like a fairyland.

韩　佳：大牛，这就是摄身岩了。在这里运气好的话，可以看见佛光。

大　牛：佛光，这佛光指的是什么呢？这里是不是有一座佛像会发光吗？

韩　佳：不是，不是。这个佛光又叫峨眉宝光。当你人站在这里，背对着太阳的
　　　　时候，你会看见你面前的云雾中，有一个彩色的光环，而你的身影就在
　　　　这个光环的中间。

大　牛：这么神奇啊！哎，这光环中只有一个人吗？

韩　佳：对呀。即使是成千成万个人一起看，光环中也只有一个人。④

大　牛：真神奇啊！要是我能亲眼看见就好了。⑤

韩　佳：佛光可不是轻易能看见的。有佛光的日子一年之中也只有70多次。一般
　　　　会在下午的两点到四点之间出现，所以很难得的。

124

Daniel: It's really a beautiful place like a fairyland.

Han Jia: Daniel, this is Sheshen Yan. If you have luck, you can see Buddha's halo.

Daniel: Buddha's halo. What is Buddha's halo? Is there a Buddhist temple that can give off light?

Han Jia: No. It doesn't mean that. Buddha's halo is also called Emei magic light. If you're standing here when the sun is behind you, you can see a colourful luminous ring in the clouds before you and your body figure is right in the middle of the luminous ring.

Daniel: How magic it is! Yes. Is there only one figure in the luminous ring?

Han Jia: Yes. Even there are thousands of people standing there, there is only one figure in the luminous ring.

Daniel: How magic it is! If only I could see it for myself.

Han Jia: It's not easy for you to see Buddha's halo. There are only 70 days in a year, when you can see Buddha's halo. Generally speaking, Buddha's halo appears between two to four o'clock in the afternoon. So it's really a rare event.

韩　佳：其实峨眉山不光有着最著名的四大奇观，我发现这儿至少还有四绝呢。

大　牛：还有四绝？

韩　佳：嗯，这其中有一绝人家可以不看，你大牛啊，非看不可。⑥

大　牛：我不能不看，那是什么呢？

韩　佳：想看啊，明天就知道了。

大　牛：嗨，这韩佳又卖关子了。没关系，我们先轻松一下。看看峨眉山的美景，
　　　　说不定她说的四绝还在里面呢。

Han Jia: In fact I've noticed there are not only the well-known four Wonders, but also at least four uniques here.

Daniel: Four uniques?

Han Jia: Yes. For one of the four uniques, others may not go and see it. you have to see it.

Daniel: I have to see it. What is it?

Han Jia: If you want to see it, you'll get to know it tomorrow.

Daniel: Hi, Han Jia is again keeping me guessing. It's all right. Let's relax for a while and have a look at the beautiful scenes of Mt Emei. Maybe the four uniques are among them.

生词 Words and Expression

1.	文化	（名）	wénhuà	culture
2.	遗产	（名）	yíchǎn	legacy, heritage
3.	仙境	（名）	xiānjìng	fairyland
4.	一般	（形）	yìbān	general
5.	奇妙	（形）	qímiào	wonderful
6.	即使…也…		jíshǐ…yě…	even if. . .
7.	要是…就…		yàoshi…jiù…	if. . .
8.	难得	（形）	nándé	rare
9.	卖关子		mài guānzi	to keep people in suspense or in guessing

注释 Notes

1. 你倒是说说峨眉山有哪些奇妙的景观……

这里"倒是"是副词，表示追问或催促。

The expression"倒是"is used as an adverb here, expressing the idea to urge somebody to do something.

例如：你倒是说句话呀，你去还是不去？

2. 先从第一奇观看起，一个一个看。

汉语里，数词"一"加量词可以重叠，在句中作状语，表示动作的方式。

In Chinese, numeral"一"followed by a measure word can be repeated and used in a sentence as an adverbial, showing the manner of an action.

例如：书要一本一本看，不能同时看几本书。

3. 这里好冷啊。

"好"这里是副词，表示程度深，"很"的意思。

"好"is an adverb here, meaning"very","rather"and etc.

例如：他的眼睛好大啊。

4. 即使是成千成万个人在一起看，光环中也只有一个人。

"即使……也……"这是一个让步复句，连词"即使"引出某种事实作出假设的让步，关联词"也"引出正面的意思。

"即使… 也…" is equivalent to "Even if…" in English, which is a concession complex sentence, and "也" leads to the main clause.

例如：工作上即使有困难，你也要想办法去克服。

5. 要是我能亲眼看见就好了。

"要是……就……"这是一个假设复句，连词"要是"引出一种假设，关联词"就"引出在这种情况下会出现的结果。

"要是… 就…" is equivalent to "if…" in English, which is a supposition complex sentence, and "就" leads to the main clause. "要是" introduces a supposition while "就" introduces the result that may be led to under the supposition.

例如：明天要是下雨，我们就不出去了。

6. 非看不可

"非……不……"表示一定要这样，"非"后面常是动词，"不……"常常是"不可、不行、不成"。

The structure is used in a sentence meaning "must", which is followed by a verb; and "不…" is often followed by "可"，"行" or "成" forming phrases "不可，不行，不成".

例如：听你这一介绍，我明天非去不可。

替换练习 Substitution Drills

1. 峨眉山	是	世界	文化遗产	之一。
长江			最大的河流	
上海			有名的大城市	
中国			文明古国	

129

2. 峨眉山的美景　　谁都知道。
   中国的长城
   苏州的园林
   杭州的龙井茶

3. 这里　　　　真是太美了，　　像　　仙镜　　　　　一样。
   这里的生活　　　　　　　　　　　　神仙的生活
   那边的风景　　　　　　　　　　　　画儿
   这儿的天空　　　　　　　　　　　　蓝色的大海

会话 Conversation

完成下列会话　Complete the following dialogues
（如括号里有词语或提示，请按要求做　Use words or phrases in the brackets）

A: 听说峨眉山是世界文化遗产，你知道吗?
B: _____。（谁）
A: 山上的美景不少吧。
B: 那当然。其中有两个_____。（非…不…）

A: 外面冷不冷?
B: _____。（好）
A: 穿上棉衣怎么样?
B: _____。（即使…也…）

峨眉山

【第二集】

场景 峨眉山山路

大　牛：哎，韩佳，昨天你说峨眉有一绝。我一定要去看看，是什么呀？

韩　佳：我说的是峨眉山著名的一景——黑白二水洗牛心。

大　牛：牛心啊？这我一定要去看看。

场景 牛心石

韩　佳：大牛，你看，牛心在那儿呢。

大　牛：啊，原来是一块石头。

韩　佳：对啊。这块石头就叫牛心石。

大　牛：是很像一颗心啊。

韩　佳：这牛心石就是典型的玄武岩，就是我所说的峨眉山的第一绝了。

大　牛：哦，玄武岩。这里的地质分布非常奇特。

韩　佳：没错。峨眉山的玄武岩分布广泛，外形奇特，而且经历了许多个不同时代的沉积，所以呀，有很高的研究价值。峨眉山有地质博物馆的美誉。

Éméi Shān yǒu "Dìzhì Bówùguǎn" de měiyù.

峨眉山有"地质博物馆"的美誉。

Mt. Emei is acclaimed as a geological museum.

Daniel: Yesterday you said there was a unique thing on Mt. Emei that I must see. What is it?

Han Jia: What I said is one of the renowned scenic spots on Mt. Emei. It is "hei bai er shui xi niu xin" (Two springs wash over an ox-heart-shaped rock).

Daniel: An ox heart? I must go and have a look.

Han Jia: Daniel, the "niu xin" is right over there.

Daniel: Oh, it's actually a rock.

Han Jia: Yes. This rock is called "Niuxinshi" (an ox-heart-shaped rock).

Daniel: It does look like a heart.

Han Jia: This "Niuxinshi" rock is typical basalt. This is what I called the first unique thing of Mt. Emei.

Daniel: Oh, a basalt rock. It seems the geology here is very special.

Han Jia: Absolutely. The basaltic deposits are widely distributed on Mt. Emei and take bizarre formations. The rocks here have undergone various stages of sedimentation. So they are very valuable for scientific studies. Mt. Emei is acclaimed as a "geological museum".

峨眉山

大　牛：韩佳，你不是说要带我去看峨嵋山第二绝吗？②怎么喝起茶来了？③

韩　佳：你先品品峨眉山的名茶——竹叶青，听我给你摆摆龙门阵。

大　牛：这茶是不错，可是喝茶要打仗啊？还要摆阵啊？

Wǒ gěi nǐ bǎi lóngménzhèn.

我　给　你　摆　龙门阵。

I'll tell you all about it.

韩　佳：在四川人们管聊天不叫"说"，也不叫"侃"，而叫"摆"，④意思就是铺开来说。摆龙门阵就是天南海北侃侃而谈。这是四川特有的一个词。你说算不算一绝呢？

大　牛：嗯。够绝的。

韩　佳：而且四川人摆龙门阵，通常都要泡上一壶好茶，坐在风景秀美的环境中，就像我们现在这样。

大　牛：我看你也够能摆的了。这龙门阵我早就听明白了。咱们赶紧去看峨眉山第三绝吧。

韩　佳：好啊，走吧。

大　牛：走。

Daniel: Han Jia, did you say you would take me to see the second unique thing of Mt. Emei? Why are you drinking tea here?

Han Jia: You'd better have a taste of the renowned tea of Mt. Emei−Zhuyeqing first. Then I'll tell you a story.

Daniel: This tea isn't bad. But why do you want to put up a fight when we drink tea here? (Bai longmenzhen: originally to deploy troops in line with the Dragon Gate Tactic. Sichuan slang meaning to tell yarns) I'll have a chat (or tell yarns) with you.

Han Jia: In Sichuan, people don't call chat "shuo", or "kan". Instead, they use "bai", originally meaning to spread things out, to mean to tell something at length. "Bai longmenzhen" means to talk about all sorts of things leisurely. This is a phrase peculiar to Sichuan people. Don't you think it's one of the unique things here?

Daniel: Yes, it's absolutely unique.

Han Jia: And when Sichuan people want to have a chat, they usually brew a pot of good tea and sit in a beautiful environment just like we do now.

Daniel: In my opinion, you are quite good at telling yarns. Now I'm clear about "longmenzhen". We'd better go see the third unique thing of Mt. Emei.

Han Jia: All right, let's go.

Daniel: Let's go.

韩 佳：这第三绝我还得给你摆。

大 牛：啊？还摆啊？

韩 佳：我要是不摆，你听都没听说过，看见了你
也不认识。

大 牛：哈，有什么东西我大牛能没听说过，不认
识？

韩 佳：鸽子树，你听说过吗？

大 牛：鸽子树？谁没听说过？不就是一种，一种鸽
子喜欢栖息的树嘛？

韩 佳：说你不知道吧，你还不承认。

大 牛：那你说是什么树啊？

韩 佳：鸽子树学名叫珙桐，之所以叫鸽子树，是
因为它的花朵都是白色的，而且一对一对
地长在一起，很像白鸽躲在树叶中一样。

大 牛：哦，原来你说的是那个鸽子树啊。早说嘛，
太普通了。

韩 佳：这珙桐是一千多万年前的树种。

Gǒngtóng shì yì qiān duō wàn nián qián de shùzhǒng.
珙 桐 是 一 千 多 万 年 前 的 树 种。

The dove tree is a kind of tree which was present over ten
million years ago.

Han Jia: I'll tell you, in detail, about the third unique thing here.

Daniel: Oh, will you?

Han Jia: If I don't, you'll never know about it. Even if you see it, you won't know what it is.

Daniel: There is nothing I haven't heard of, or I don't know.

Han Jia: Have you ever heard of the dove tree?

Daniel: Dove tree? Everyone knows about it. Is it a kind of tree on which pigeons like to perch?

Han Jia: As I said you knew nothing about it, but you refuse to admit.

Daniel: Then tell me what kind of tree it is?

Han Jia: The scientific name of the tree is called gongtong tree. It is called a dove tree because its flowers are all whiteand grow in pairs, just like doves hiding among the leaves.

Daniel: Oh, actually you mean dove trees. You should have told me about it earlier. It's common knowledge.

Han Jia: The dove tree is a kind of tree which has existed for over ten million years.

韩　佳：大牛，你看，这就是第四绝了。

大　牛：哦，原来第四绝就是滑竿哪。

韩　佳：你还知道滑竿哪。这"滑竿"用英文怎么说呢？

大　牛：那就是 bamboo sedan chair。

韩　佳：咱们也去试试吧。

大　牛：好，感受一下峨眉山第四绝。啊，坐滑竿果然很舒服啊，是吧，韩佳？

韩　佳：可不是吗？⑤舒服。

场景 吊桥

韩　佳：好了，观众朋友们，今天我们节目结束的时间又快到了。其实说到这奇
　　　　妙之处，峨眉山有那么多的奇观美景，这本身也是一绝啊！

大　牛：嗯，对。现在我们轻松一下，欣赏峨眉山的美妙景色吧。

Han Jia: Daniel, look, this is the fourth unique thing.

Daniel: Oh, actually it's "huagan" .

Han Jia: You do know a bamboo sedan chair. How do you say "huagan" in English?

Daniel: That is bamboo sedan chair.

Han Jia: Let's go and have a try.

Daniel: Good, and have an experience of the fourth unique thing of Mt. Emei. Oh, it's really comfortable to sit in a bamboo sedan chair. How do you feel, Han Jia?

Han Jia: Really comfortable.

Han Jia: Okay, everyone, it's about time to conclude our program for toady. Actually, when we talk about the mountain's marvelous beauty, Mt. Emei is full of such scenic spots, which itself is another instance of the uniqueness of this mountain.

Daniel: Oh, yes. Now, let's relax for a while and enjoy the wonderful sights of Mt. Emei.

生词 Words and Expressions

1.	绝	（名）	jué	something unique
2.	原来	（形、副）	yuánlái	It turns out...
3.	典型	（形）	diǎnxíng	characteristic
4.	研究	（动）	yánjiū	to study
5.	地质	（名）	dìzhì	geology
6.	博物馆	（名）	bówùguǎn	museum
7.	品茶		pǐn chá	to sample tea
8.	天南海北		tiān nán hǎi běi	all over the place (country)

注释 Notes

1. 原来**是块石头。**

   这里"原来"是副词，发现从前不知道的情况，含有恍然大悟的意思。

   In Chinese "原来" is an adverb, which means in English "it turns out...".

   例如：我以为他是中国人呢，原来他是日本人啊。

2. 你**不是**说要带我去看峨眉山的第二绝**吗？**

   "不是…吗"是汉语反问句的一种句式，强调肯定。

   "不是…吗" is a form of rhetoric questions in Chinese, and used for emphasis.

   例如：你不是游览过长城吗？给我们简单介绍一下吧。

3. 怎么喝**起**茶**来**了？

   复合趋向补语"起来"放在动词"喝"的后边，表示喝的动作开始并有继续下去的意思，动词如带有宾语，宾语要放在"起来"之间。

   The structure "起 ... 来" follows the verb "喝" here, expressing the action "喝" has started and is likely to go on. If the verb takes an object, the object should be put in between "起" and "来".

   例如：你们听，孩子们唱起歌来了。

4. 人们管聊天不叫"说"，也不叫"侃"，而叫"摆"

这里"而"是连词，表示转折，"而"前后两部分，一部分肯定一部分否定，对比说明一件事。

"而" is a conjunction indicating transition. The two parts "而" connects can be either affirmative or negative, used to explain the whole situation.

例如：看来这事儿已经不是一个小问题而是一个大问题了。

5. 可不是吗？

"可不是吗"表示同意对方的话，也可以说"可不是"、"可不"。

"可不是吗" is used to express agreement, roughly meaning "Isn't that so?" or the like in English. "可不是", "可不" can also be used instead.

例如：A: 我们有好几年没见面了吧。

B: 可不是，大概有四五年没见面了。

替换练习 Substitution Drills

1. 峨眉山	有	地质博物馆	的	美誉。
他		人民艺术家		
李先生		足球先生		
她		电影皇后		

2. 我给你	摆	.	龙门阵。
	讲		故事
	做		中国菜
	当		翻译

3. 珙桐	是	一千多万年	前的	树种。
这座寺庙		一千多年		建筑
这本小说		一百多年		文学著作
那张画儿		五百多年		作品

会话 Conversation

完成下列会话　Complete the following dialogues
（如括号里有词语或提示，请按要求做　Use words or phrases in the brackets）

A: 你说山上有一景点我们非看不可，在哪儿啊？

B: 就在这儿啊！

A: 什么？你说了半天 _____。（原来）

B: 别着急啊，我们先看看，看完你再说。

• •

A: 这种树叫什么名字？

B: 这里的老百姓 _____。（管…叫…）

A: 这是一种珍贵树种吧。

B: _____。（可不是）

峨眉山

【第三集】

大　牛：哎，韩佳。你这手里拿着什么呢？

韩　佳：猴子啊。提到峨眉山可不能不说一说这些可爱的小家伙们。①

大　牛：为什么呢？

韩　佳：你不知道吧？猴子是峨眉山的吉祥物。

Hóu zi shì É méi Shān de jíxiángwù.

猴子 是 峨眉 山 的 吉祥物。

The monkey is Mount Emei's lucky charm.

韩　佳：这猴子是峨眉山的吉祥物。

大　牛：哦，以前我还真不知道。

韩　佳：那今天我和大牛就要带您到峨眉山上去看一看那些可爱的小家伙们。

大　牛：走了，去看看。

Daniel: Han Jia? What's in your hand?

Han Jia: A monkey. When we talk about Mt. Emei, we can't help saying something about these lovely creatures.

Daniel: Why?

Han Jia: You may not know it. Monkey is the mascot of Mt. Emei. The monkey is Mount Emei's mascot.

Han Jia: Monkey is the mascot of Mt. Emei.

Daniel: Oh, I didn't know it before.

Han Jia: Today, Daniel and I will take you to Mt. Emei to have look at these lovely creatures.

Daniel: Let's go and take a look.

大　牛：峨眉山自然生态猴区。哎，韩佳，咱们这就进入了猴子的领地了吧?

韩　佳：对啊。峨眉山是全国最大的自然生态猴区。听说这儿的猴子多着呢，活泼机灵，而且还不怕人。

Zhèr　de　hóuzi　huópo　jīling.

这儿　的　猴子　活泼　机灵。

The monkeys here are lively and intelligent.

大　牛：不怕人呢。嗯，那就太好了。这次到了峨眉山，我来多交几个好朋友。

Daniel: The Mt. Emei Natural and Ecological Habitat for Monkeys. Hey, Han Jia, we've thus entered the monkeys' domain?

Han Jia: Yes. Mt. Emei is the country's biggest natural and ecological habitat for monkeys. I heard there are many monkeys here. They are lively, clever and not afraid of people. The monkeys here are lively and clever.

Daniel: They aren't afraid of people? That's great. This time on Mt. Emei, I'd like to make a more friends with them.

韩　佳：哎，大牛，都说峨眉山上猴子多，怎么一只也没见着啊？

大　牛：是啊。奇怪。我知道了，肯定是因为有一只厉害的猴子来了，所以山上
　　　　的猴子都躲起来了。

韩　佳：厉害的猴子？

大　牛：嗯。

韩　佳：在哪儿呢？

大　牛：远在天边，近在眼前。

韩　佳：嗨，你个大牛！昨天刚知道我属猴，②今天就拿我开玩笑。

大　牛：嗨，这山上没有猴子也不错嘛。你想想中国不是有句话嘛："山中无老
　　　　虎，猴子称大王。"现在你可以来一个，"山中无猴子，韩佳称大王。"

Han Jia: It's said there are many monkeys on Mt. Emei. But why we haven't seen even a single one yet?

Daniel: Yes, it's strange. I am sure the reason must be because of the presence of a ferocious monkey. So all the other monkeys here have fled into hiding.

Han Jia: A ferocious monkey?

Daniel: Yes.

Han Jia: Where is it?

Daniel: It's close at hand though seemingly far away.

Han Jia: Oh, you sly Daniel! Only yesterday you learned that I was born in the Year of the Monkey, and now you are trying to make fun of me.

Daniel: Well, it wouldn't be bad if there wasn't any monkeys on the mountain. Don't you know the Chinese saying: "The monkey rules the mountain when there is no tiger"? Now Han Jia, you may try to rule the mountain when there is no monkey.

韩　佳：出来了。

大　牛：哎，我看见猴子了。来，喂它好吃的。

韩　佳：哎，能随便喂吗？

大　牛：没问题。来。

管理员：不能随便喂食物，这个不是专用猴粮。猴子吃了其他的东西容易
　　　　生病的。

大　牛：您是？

韩　佳：您是猴区管理员胡永忠先生吧？

管理员：哎。对，对，对。

韩　佳：我在电视上见过您。

大　牛：可是我不哄猴子高兴，它们怎么会
　　　　跟我交朋友呢？

管理员：来，来，来，没关系。我这里有我们专
　　　　用的食物。它这个是有安全袋的。

大　牛：哦，好。

管理员：你来试一下吧？

大　牛：哦，多省事啊。

管理员：这样既安全又卫生。③

大　牛：我要喂给猴子四袋猴粮。

韩　佳：你为什么要喂四袋啊？

Han Jia: Oh, there they come.

Daniel: I can see them now. Come on and feed them with something nice.

Han Jia: Can we feed them without permission?

Daniel: No problem. Come on.

Janitor: No, you can't feed them indiscriminately. This is not the special feed for these monkeys. Monkeys might get sick if they eat other feeds.

Daniel: Are you . . . ?

Han Jia: Are you Mr. Hu Yongzhong, keeper of the monkey zone?

Janitor: Oh, yes, yes.

Han Jia: I saw you once on TV.

Daniel: But since I don't know how to please these monkeys, how could they like to make friends with me?

Janitor: Come on. Don't worry. We have feed specially prepared for them. There are safety bags.

Daniel: Okay.

Janitor: Come on and have a try.

Daniel: It's so easy.

Janitor: It's both safe and hygienic.

Daniel: I'm going to feed them four bags of feed.

Han Jia: Why do you want to feed them four bags of feed?

大　牛：这就是朝三暮四的故事嘛。你看，现在是早晨啊，当然要喂给猴子四袋猴粮哪。

韩　佳：大牛，你很有进步嘛。朝三暮四的故事你都知道了。

大　牛：又夸我了。

韩　佳：可是人家故事里讲的不是喂猴子花生。

大　牛：哎，这花生也很有营养啊。

韩　佳：这朝三暮四啊，多指反复无常，随意变化，跟原来的用法不一样了。

大　牛：哦，我明白了。*朝三暮四形容人做事反复无常。朝三暮四。*哎，我的水呢？这只猴子啊……

韩　佳：哎！大牛咱们去跟那些猴子照张相吧。

大　牛：走。

Zánmen　gēn　zhè xiē　hóu zi　zhào　zhāng　xiàng　bā.
咱们　跟　这些　猴子　照　张　相　吧。

Let's take some photos with the monkeys.

场景　峨眉山自然生态猴区

韩　佳：观众朋友们，这些小猴子可爱吗？

大　牛：嗯，我觉得够可爱的了。④ *现在让我们轻松一下，跟峨眉山的猴子说声再见吧。*

Daniel: There is a story about the proverb "zhao san mu si". You see, this is morning time. So I should feed them four bags.

Han Jia: Daniel, you're making steady progress. You even know the story about "zhao san mu si".

Daniel: You're praising me again.

Han Jia: But in the story, the feed for the monkeys is not peanuts.

Daniel: But peanuts are more nutritious.

Han Jia: "Zhao san mu si" usually means to be capricious and keep changing one's mind all the time. The usage is different from its original meaning.

Daniel: Oh, now I'm clear about the proverb "zhao san mu si". "Zhao san mu si" is used to describe those who behave capriciously. That's "zhao san mu si". Oh, where is my water? This monkey…

Han Jia: Hey! Daniel, let's go take a picture with those monkeys.

Daniel: Okay. Let's take some pictures with the monkeys.

Han Jia: Hi, everyone. Are these little monkeys lovely?

Daniel: Yes, I think they are very lovely. Now, let's relax for a while and say hello to the monkeys of Mt. Emei.

生词 Words and Expressions

1. 猴子　　　（名）　　　hóuzi　　　monkey
2. 可爱　　　（形）　　　kěài　　　lovely
3. 吉祥物　　（名）　　　jíxiángwù　　mascot
4. 活泼　　　（形）　　　huópō　　　lively
5. 机灵　　　（形）　　　jī ling　　　clever
6. 开玩笑　　　　　　　kāi wánxiào　　to crack a joke
7. 既…又…　　　　　　jì … yòu…　　as well as. . .
8. 照相　　　　　　　　zhàoxiāng　　to take photos
9. 够　　　　（副）　　　gòu　　　enough

注释 Notes

1. **提到峨眉山可不能不说一说这些可爱的小家伙们。**

   "不能不……"这一结构表示必须应该。

   "不能不 ..." is a structure of double negation, meaning "must" or "have to".

   例如：由于买不到飞机票，我们不能不改变一下出发的日期。

2. **昨天刚知道我属猴。**

   中国民间有一种传统，用十二属相来记人的出生年，这十二属相分别用十二种动物来代表。它们的顺序为鼠、牛、虎、兔、龙、蛇、马、羊、猴、鸡、狗、猪。虎年出生的属虎，马年出生的属马。2005年是鸡年，这一年（农历）出生的人属鸡。

   There is a tradition in China that years in which people are born are named by 12 common animals: mouse, ox, tiger, rabbit, dragon, snake, horse, goat, monky, rooster, dog and pig. So a person may be born in the year of the tiger, or the year of the horse, etc. 2005 is the year of the rooster. So those who are born this year are said to "属鸡".

3. 这样**既**安全**又**卫生。

"既……又……"这一结构表示同时具有两方面的性质或情况，连接动词或形容词。

The structure "既 ... 又 ..." express something that the subject both has. Here verbs and adjectives can be used.

例如：他既是老师又是运动员。

4. 我觉得**够**可爱的了。

这里"够"是副词，常用来修饰形容词，表示程度高，句尾常有"的"。

"够"(originally, meaning "enough", but here it actually means "rather", is an adverb used to modify an adjective, expressing a high degree. And sentences with it often have "的" at the end of the sentences.)

例如：今天够冷的，屋里的温度才十二度。

替换练习 Substitution Drills

1. 猴子　　是　　峨眉山　　的　　吉祥物。
   熊猫　　　　　中国　　　　　　珍稀动物
   龙井茶　　　　西湖　　　　　　特产
   珙王同　　　　世界　　　　　　珍贵树种

2. 这儿的猴子　　活泼机灵。
   那些孩子们
   这位小朋友
   那个小姑娘

3. 咱们　　跟　　这些猴子们　　照张相吧。
   我们　　　　　老师
   你们　　　　　那些孩子们
   你　　　　　　这位外国朋友

155

会话 Conversation

完成下列会话　Complete the following dialogue
（如括号里有词语或提示，请按要求做　Use words or phrases in the brackets）

A: 你手里拿着什么？

B: _____。（游览图）

A: 给我看一下儿，山上的景点不少啊。

B: 是啊。山上的景点还 _____。（着呢）

· ·

A: 这个纪念品好看吗？

B: 好看，多少钱一个？

A: 二十块，便宜吗？

B: _____，我去买一个。（够）

乐山

【第一集】

大　牛：哎，观众朋友们，我们现在所在的位置就是距离峨眉山市三十一公里的乐山。

韩　佳：哎，大牛，一提到乐山，你首先想到的是什么呀？

大　牛：那当然是乐山大佛。

场景 乐山山顶

大　牛：哎呀，都爬到山顶上了，哪里有佛呀？①

韩　佳：大牛，看你的右边。

大　牛：啊，这么大啊。

韩　佳：可不是嘛。要不然怎么说山是一尊佛，②佛是一座山呢？乐山大佛可是以整座山为基础，历时90余年才开凿好的。

大　牛：真是太不容易了。早听说乐山大佛是世界上最大的坐佛。

"Lè　Shān　Dà　Fó"shì　shìjiè　shang　zuì　dà　de　zuòfó.
"乐　山　大　佛"是　世　界　上　最　大　的　坐佛。

The "Leshan Grand Buddha" is the largest sitting Buddha statue in the world.

韩　佳：它有71米高呢。

大　牛：啊，那相当于二十层楼那么高了。

韩　佳：你看它的耳朵，它的耳朵有7米长。我们两人的身高加起来，才是它的一半。

大　牛：哇，真是大得惊人啊！哎，韩佳，我们能下去看它的全貌吗？

韩　佳：能啊，我们走那边的栈道就可以下去了。

大　牛：走吧。

Daniel: Hey, dear audience, we are now at Leshan Mountain, 31km away from the city of Mt. Emei.

Han Jia: Hey, Daniel, speaking of Leshan Mountain, what's the first thing that comes into your mind?

Daniel: It's certainly Leshan Grand Buddha.

Daniel: Wow, we have climbed up to the top of the mountain. Where's the Buddha?

Han Jia: Daniel, look to your right.

Daniel: Wow, so big.

Han Jia: Exactly. That's why the saying goes the mountain is a Buddha and the Buddha is a mountain. Leshan Grand Buddha was carved from a whole mountain, and it took more than 90 years to finish it.

Daniel: That's really something. I've heard long time ago that Leshan Grand Buddha is the biggest sitting Buddha in the world.

Han Jia: It's 71 meters high.

Daniel: Wow. 71 metres, that's about the same height as a twenty-storey building.

Han Jia: Look at its ears. Its ears are 7 meters long. The height of the two of us is only half of it.

Daniel: Wow, that's fabulous. Hey, Han Jia, can we go down there to have a look at the complete picture?

Han Jia: Sure, let's take the plank path over there, and we can go down.

Daniel: Let's go.

韩　佳：大牛，你怎么不走了？累了吧？

大　牛：不是，不是，你看这是什么路？拐来拐去的，③弄得我晕头转向。

韩　佳：这就是有名的九曲栈道。

Zhè jiù shì yǒumíng de "Jiǔ Qū Zhàndào" a !
这 就 是 有名 的 "九 曲 栈道" 啊！

This is the famous "Nine Bend Cliff Path"!

大　牛：为什么要九曲呢？要是能两曲三曲，我就不会这么晕了。

韩　佳：也许在中国文化中，九是代表最大的数字。我们继续走吧，小心点啊。

大　牛：哎，韩佳，这乐山大佛是什么时候修建的呀？④

韩　佳：大佛是在唐代修建的。建成到现在已经有1200多年了。

大　牛：我在想它都经过了那么多年的风吹雨打，它怎么保存得这么好呢？

韩　佳：你注意到没有？大佛的发髻、衣领，还有衣服胸前的褶皱，这些雕刻
　　　　可不仅是为了美观，其实它们都是排水沟。这些排水沟组成了科学的排
　　　　水系统，这样对保护大佛起到了很重要的作用。⑤

Zhèxiē páishuǐgōu duì bǎohù Dà Fó qǐdào le zhòngyào de zuòyòng.
这些 排水沟 对 保护 大佛 起到了 重要 的 作用。

These drainage ruts have played a crucial role in preserving the Grand Buddha.

Han Jia: Daniel, why do you stop? Are you tired?

Daniel: No, no, look, what kind of road is it? So many twists and turns. I am confused and disoriented.

Han Jia: It's the famous Nine Turns Plank Path.

Daniel: Why nine turns? If it only has several turns, I won't be so confused.

Han Jia: Maybe in Chinese culture, nine is the biggest figure. Oh, let's go on. Be careful.

Daniel: Hey, Han Jia, when was Leshan Grand Buddha built?

Han Jia: It was built in the Tang Dynasty. It has been more than 1, 200 years since its completion.

Daniel: I am thinking it has gone through a lot of wind and rain, how can it be kept in such a good condition?

Han Jia: Did you notice the Buddha's hair, collar, and the folds on the clothes on the chest? They are not just decoration. In fact, they are gutters. These gutters form a scientific drainage system. They play an important role in protecting the Buddha.

大　牛：韩佳，你说要是我也留这么一个发型，衣服上还有那么多的褶皱，那下雨天是不是不用打伞了？

韩　佳：人家那是巧夺天工。大牛，你这个是异想天开。

大　牛：异想天开，什么意思？

韩　佳：异想天开也是一个成语。用来形容想法非常奇特，但事实上却是办不到的。

大　牛：刚才开个玩笑。

韩　佳：好了，观众朋友们，我们今天节目结束的时间又快到了。乐山大佛可真称得上是中国古代人智慧的结晶了。

大　牛：现在让我们再来好好地看看这世界上最大的石刻坐佛。

Daniel: Han Jia, do you think that if I have such a hairstyle and have so many folds on my clothes, I won't need umbrella in rain anymore?

Han Jia: Those on the Buddha are wonderful workmanship excelling nature. Daniel, you are indulging yourself in the wildest fantasy.

Daniel: What does "Yi xiang tian kai" mean?

Han Jia: "Yi xiang tian kai" is an idiom too. It means the thought is whimsical, and can never be realized in fact.

Daniel: I was kidding just now.

Han Jia: All right, dear audience, it's time to say good-bye again. Leshan Grand Buddha is really the essence of ancient Chinese wisdom.

Daniel: Let's take a closer look at the biggest stone sitting Buddha in the world.

生词 Words and Expressions

1.	耳朵	（名）	ěrduo	ear(s)
2.	栈道	（名）	zhàndào	a plank roadway
3.	也许	（副）	yěxǔ	perhaps, maybe
4.	小心	（形）	xiǎoxīn	careful
5.	修建	（动）	xiūjiàn	to build
6.	保存	（动）	bǎocún	to keep
7.	重要	（形）	zhòngyào	important
8.	作用	（名）	zuòyòng	role

注释 Notes

1. **哪里有佛啊？**

   这里疑问代词"哪里"用于反问，目的在于否定。

   "哪里" is used in rhetoric questions for negation.

   例如：昨天的事他哪里知道啊，他今天刚到。

2. **要不然怎么说山是一尊佛。**

   现代汉语中，数词一般不能直接与名词连用，中间要有量词，不同的名词往往有自己特定的量词。这里"尊"是佛的特定量词。

   Generally, in modern Chinese, when a numeral is used with a noun, there should be a measure word in between, and different nouns take different measure words. Here "尊" is a measure word specially used for Buddhist statue.

3. **拐来拐去的。**

   "动词 + 来 + 动词 + 去"表示动作的多次重复。

   The structure "verb + 来 + verb + 去" is used to show the action is repeated many times.

   例如：我想来想去，最后还是决定去中国学汉语。

4. 这 "乐山大佛" 是什么时候修建的呀?

当一个动作在过去发生，而我们现在要着重指出那个动作发生的时间、地点、方式等，就可以用 "是……的" 这种结构。

The structure "是 ... 的" is used to point out emphatically the time, place or manner when an action takes place.

例如: 这房子是 1998 年修建的（时间）

我是从北京来的（地点）

他们是坐飞机去的（方式）

5. 这样对保护大佛起到了重要作用。

这里动词 "起" 是 "发生" 的意思，可带 "了、着、过"，常用 "作用" 作宾语。

"起 ... 作用" means to "play a role in...". It may take "了，着，过".

例如: 你是哥哥，在弟弟妹妹面前应起模范带头作用。

替换练习 Substitution Drills

1. "乐山大佛"	是	世界上	最	大	的	坐佛。
这座园林		中国		大		园林
长江		中国		长		河流
这座桥		中国		古老		桥梁

2. 这就是有名的 "九曲栈道"	啊!
杭州西湖	
八达岭长城	
皇家园林颐和园	

3. 这些排水沟	对	保护大佛	起到了重要作用。
这些树		保护环境	
这些做法		提高大家的汉语水平	
那样做		保护世界文化遗产	

会话 Conversation

完成下列会话　Complete the following dialogues
（如括号里有词语或提示，请按要求做　Use words or phrases in the brackets）

A: ＿＿＿＿＿＿＿＿＿＿＿？（怎么）

B: 我在等他们。

A: 你们来了好几天了吧?

B: ＿＿＿＿＿＿＿＿＿＿＿我们是昨天刚到的。（哪儿）

• •

A: 你们住的那个饭店怎么样?

B: 不错，服务很好。＿＿＿＿＿＿＿＿＿＿？（是…的）

A: 那个饭店是去年建的。

B: 虽然不是五星级饭店，但 ＿＿＿＿＿＿＿＿＿。（比）

乐山

【第二集】

大　牛：观众朋友们，你们来过这里吗？四川的乐山港码头。我们一会儿就要坐
　　　　船了。

韩　佳：赶紧走吧，船要开了。

场景 船上（古城墙）

韩　佳：大牛，你看那边。

大　牛：像是我以前见过的城墙。

韩　佳：对，是这个地方，古代的城墙。它呀，是用坚固的红砂条石砌成的。

大　牛：城墙的作用就是防御敌人，所以得修得坚固一些。

韩　佳：你呀，只说对了一点。还有一点呢？你看，这城墙外边是什么？

大　牛：哦，江水。坚固的城墙还可以用来防洪水。

韩　佳：嗯，你看它经历了几百年江水的冲刷，还那么坚固呢。

大　牛：是啊，咱们上去看看吧。

韩　佳：好啊！

Daniel: Dear audience, have you ever been here before? Leshan Pier in Sichuan Province. We will take a boat very soon.

Han Jia: Hurry up. The boat is leaving.

Han Jia: Daniel, look over there.

Daniel: It looks like the city wall I've seen before.

Han Jia: Right, it's the ancient city wall. It was made of solid red sandstone.

Daniel: It's for keeping the enemy off. So it must be built very solid.

Han Jia: You just mentioned one reason. There is another one. Look, what's on the outside of the city wall?

Daniel: Oh! The river, so the wall was also usedto prevent flooding.

Han Jia: Right, see, it has gone through river for hundreds of years, but it's still so firm.

Daniel: Right, let's go up there and take a look.

Han Jia: All right.

船上（巨型睡佛）

大　牛：韩佳，你看我们已经离山够远的了，乐山大佛都变得那么小了。

韩　佳：离开了山中的佛，才能看到更大的佛呀。

大　牛：乐山大佛不是最大的吗？怎么有更大的？

韩　佳：你看，那边的山像不像一个人在睡觉啊？①

Nà biān de Shān xiàng bú xiàng yí gè rén zài shuì jiào?
那边 的 山 像 不 像 一 个 人 在 睡觉？

Do you think the mountains over there look like someone sleeping?

韩　佳：那就是有名的巨型睡佛。从头到脚一共有 1500 多米长呢。②你说能不能
称得上是巨型啊？

大　牛：是啊，从这里我就能很清楚地看到它的额头、鼻子，还有嘴巴。

Daniel: Han Jia, look, we've been far away from the mountain. Leshan Grand Buddha seems so small.

Han Jia: Departing from the Buddha in the mountain, then you can see a bigger Buddha.

Daniel: Isn't Leshan Grand Buddha the biggest? Why is there something bigger?

Han Jia: Look at the mountain over there. Doesn't it look like a man sleeping?

Han Jia: That's the well-known Giant Lying Buddha. He's over 1, 500 meters from head to toe. Don't you think it can be called "giant"?

Daniel: Yes, I can see him clearly here. I saw his forehead, nose and mouth.

韩　佳：大牛，你看那儿。

大　牛：啊，那不是咱们昨天去过的乐山大佛吗？

韩　佳：没错。乐山大佛正好端坐在巨型睡佛的胸部，所以这样就形成了佛中有佛的奇观了。

大　牛：哎，对了，提起乐山大佛，我昨天忘了问你，古代人为什么要在这里开凿乐山大佛呢？

Gǔdàirén wèishénme yào zài zhè li kāizáo "Lè Shān Dà Fó" ne?

古代人 为什么 要 在 这里 开凿 "乐 山 大 佛" 呢？

Why did the ancient Chinese decide to construct the Grand Buddha here?

韩　佳：因为这个地方是岷江、青衣江、大渡河三江的汇合之处，自古风高浪急，经常有翻船的。为了保佑这些船只，前后有三个志向相同的人，毫无保留地献出了他们所有的财产和毕生的精力，历时90余年，终于开凿了这世界第一的石刻大佛。大牛，别光顾着看山啊，也欣赏欣赏这儿的水啊。

大　牛：哎呀，这个地方不仅山奇水也美。

韩　佳：那当然了，你可别忘了这里可是三江汇合的地方，难得啊！

Zhè li kě shì sān jiāng huìhé de dìfang a!

这里 可 是 三 江 汇合 的 地方 啊！

This is the place where three rivers converge!

Han Jia: Daniel, look.

Daniel: Wow. Isn't it the Leshan Grand Buddha we visited yesterday?

Han Jia: Exactly. Leshan Grand Buddha is sitting right on the chest of the Giant Lying Buddha. So it forms a marvelous spectacle of Buddha inside Buddha.

Daniel: Hey, speaking of Leshan Grand Buddha, I forgot to ask you yesterday. Why did people in ancient times carve Leshan Grand Buddha here?

Han Jia: Because Min River, Qingyi River and Dadu River converge here. In ancient times, the strong wind and huge tide often overthrew many boats. To bless these boats, three men who had the same will devoted all their property and energy. It took over 90 years to carve the biggest stone Buddha in the world. Daniel, don't just look at the mountain. Enjoy the water here too.

Han Jia: Wow, the mountain is marvelous and so is the water here.

Han Jia: No doubt about it. Don't forget that the three rivers converge here. It is very rare.

大　牛：这里是三江汇合的地方。这里的山美水也美。这就叫美不胜收啊。

韩　佳：行啊，大牛，有进步啊。"美不胜收"这个成语是指美好的东西太多了，一时看不过来的意思。③

大　牛：嗯，没错，"美不胜收"是一个成语，意思是美好的东西太多了，一时看不过来。

韩　佳：好了，观众朋友们，我们今天节目结束的时间又快到了，就要离开美丽的乐山了。节目的最后让我们再去欣赏一下这儿的奇观美景吧。

Daniel: The three rivers converge here. The mountain is beautiful here, so is the water. There are so many wonderful things here.

Han Jia: Good, Daniel, you have made progress. The idiom "mei bu sheng shou" means there are so many wonderful things that you can not take them in at the same time.

Daniel: Right, "mei bu sheng shou" is a Chinese idiom which means that there is too much beautiful scenery, but not enough time to see it all.

Han Jia: All right, dear audience, it's time to say good-bye again. We will soon leave the At the end of the program, let's go beautiful Leshan Mountain and enjoy the wonderful sights here once again.

生词 Words and Expressions

1.	船	（名）	chuán	boat
2.	赶紧	（副）	gǎnjǐn	hurriedly, hastily;
3.	坚固	（形）	jiāngù	firm and strong
4.	睡觉	（动）	shuìjiào	to sleep
5.	从…到…		cóng…dào…	from. . . to. . .
6.	清楚	（形）	qīngchǔ	clear
7.	汇合	（动）	huìhé	converge, join
8.	为了	（介）	wèile	for, in order to, in order that
9.	开凿	（动）	kāizáo	to cut
10.	终于	（副）	zhōngyú	finally, at last

注释 Notes

1. **那边的山像不像一个人在睡觉啊?**

   这里"在"是副词，"正在"的意思，表示动作在进行中或状态在持续中。

   Here "在" is an adverb meaning that an action is going on or the state is continous.

   例如：他在吃饭，你等他一会儿。

   有关"正在"的用法，请参看本书第10课。

   For the usage of "在"， please refer to Lesson 10 to the book.

2. **从头到脚一共有1500多米长呢。**

   "从……到……"这一结构，"从"表示起点，"到"表示终点，常与表示时间、地点词语组合。

   The structure "从 ... 到 ..." often appears together with time expressions "从" indicates the staring point while "到" indicates the ending point.

例如：每天下午从四点到五点我们锻炼身体。

从教室到宿舍你大概要走 10 分钟。

雨不停地下着，今天我们不能去游泳了。

3. 一时看不过来

"动词 + 不过来"表示不能很好地做完某件事。

"Verb + 不过来" express the idea that something cannot be done as expected/required.

例如：这么多好书，我都看不过来了。

替换练习 Substitution Drills

1.	那边的山	像不像	一	个人在	睡觉。
	那边的景点		两		下棋
	山上那几棵树		几		聊天
	河边的景点		一		洗衣服

2.	古代人	为什么要在这里	开凿	乐山大佛？
	他们		研究	这些树种
	古代人		修建	长城
	外国人		建	别墅

3.	这里可是	三江汇合的地方	啊。
		自然生态保护区	
		世界文化遗产	
		世界地质公园	

会话 Conversation

完成下列会话　Complete the following dialogues
（如括号里有词语或提示，请按要求做　Use words or phrases in the brackets）

　　A: 你们去过北京吗?

　　B: ＿＿＿＿＿＿＿＿＿＿＿。（过）

　　A: 听说北京有很多名胜古迹，是吗?

　　B: 没错，参观一星期＿＿＿＿＿＿＿＿。（过来）

・・・・・・・・・・・・・・・・・・・・・・・・・・・・

　　A: 王小姐她们呢?

　　B: ＿＿＿＿＿＿＿＿＿＿＿＿。（在）

　　A: 照完相让她们找我一下儿，好吗?

　　B: 没问题。

附录：重点句索引
Appendix: Index of Key Sentences

第一课

1. 我们要像保护眼睛一样保护环境。

   We should take care of our environment with the same care as we protect our eyes.

2. 这里处处体现环保精神。

   The environmental awareness is evident in all of our surroundings.

3. 九寨沟里面的美景还多着呢。

   There are still many more scenic spots to be seen in Jiuzhaigou.

第二课

1. 那块大岩石像不像一张姑娘的脸？

   Does that cliff face look like a young girl's face?

2. 还有比湖水更好看的呢。

   There are sights even better than these lakes.

3. 入乡随俗

   When in Rome, do as the Romans do.

第三课

1. 五颜六色

   colorful

2. 栩栩如生

   strikingly realistic

3. 它们在这里自由自在地生活。

   They live freely here.

第四课

1. 这图案多精致啊！

   This pattern is exquisite.

2．祝福大家平安幸福。

To wish everyone peace and happiness.

3．酥油茶是藏族的传统饮料。

Buttered tea is a traditional Tibetan drink.

第五课

1．树干被水冲出了一个槽。

The water has bored a trough in the tree trunk.

2．这间小屋是个磨坊。

This small room is a mill.

3．哈达是藏族同胞心中的吉祥之物。

A Hada is a lucky charm in the eyes of the Tibetans.

第六课

1．黄龙最最吸引人的是它的颜色。

The most attractive aspect of Huanglong is its many colors.

2．这种金黄色是黄龙的地质特点。

This kind of golden color is a geological trait specific to Huanglong.

3．今天我可是大开眼界啊！

I really broadened my horizons today.

第七课

1．我这就带你看看棕色色调的景色去。

Now I'll take you to see some scenery of a brownish hue.

2．如果不是亲眼所见，很难让人相信。

If I haven't seen it with my own eyes, I'd find it hard to believe.

3．他们是一对恋人。

They are a pair of lovers.

第八课

1．这里有一千五百多种高等植物。

There are over 1,500 different kinds of higher plants located here.

2．这里的空气好，没有污染。

The air here is great, completely without pollution.

3．能在这里生活、工作，我觉得很幸运。

I feel very lucky to be able to live and work here.

第九课

1．素花湖是牟尼沟最美的湖泊之一。

Suhua Lake is one of the most beautiful lakes.

2．你快帮我在这里拍张照片吧。

Quick! Help me take a photo here.

3．这里的景色比天宫还要美。

The scenery here is more beautiful than that of the kingdom of heaven.

第十课

1．我骑马的技术还是不错的。

My equestrian skills aren't bad.

2．晚上大家都要住在自己搭的帐篷里。

In the evening, everyone has to live in the tent which they pitched by themselves.

3．我觉得这里比五星级酒店还要好。

I think that here is even better than a five-star hotel.

第十一课

1．峨眉山是世界文化遗产之一。

Mount Emei belongs to our World Cultural Heritages.

2．峨眉山的美景谁都知道。

Everyone knows of Mt. Emei's beautiful scenery.

3．这里真是太美了，像仙境一样。

It's so beautiful here, like a fairyland.

第十二课

1．峨眉山有地质博物馆的美誉。

Mt. Emei is acclaimed as a "geological museum".

2. 我给你摆龙门阵。

  I'll tell you all about it.

3. 珙王同是一千多万年前的树种。

  The dove tree is a kind of tree was present over ten million years ago.

第十三课

1. 猴子是峨眉山的吉祥物。

  The monkey is Mt. Emei's lucky charm.

2. 这儿的猴子活泼机灵。

  Monkeys here are lively and intelligent.

3. 咱们跟这些猴子照张相吧。

  Let us take a photo with the monkeys.

第十四课

1. "乐山大佛"是世界上最大的坐佛。

  "The Leshan Grand Buddha" is the largest sitting Buddha statue in the world.

2. 这就是有名的"九曲栈道"啊！

  This is the famous "Nine bend Cliff Path"!

3. 这些排水沟对保护大佛起到了重要作用。

  These drainage ruts have played a crucial role in preserving the Grand Buddha.

第十五课

1. 那边的山像不像一个人在睡觉？

  Do you think the mountains over there look like someone sleeping?

2. 古代人为什么要在这里开凿乐山大佛呢？

  Why did ancient Chinese decide to construct the Grand Buddha here?

3. 这里可是三江汇合的地方啊！

  This is the place where three rivers converge.